KAIZEN
STRATEGIES
— FOR —
WINNING
THROUGH
PEOPLE

改 善

KAI   ZEN

change   +   good

=

improvement

KAIZEN STRATEGIES
FOR
WINNING THROUGH PEOPLE

How to create a
human resources program for
competitiveness & profitability

SHEILA CANE

PITMAN PUBLISHING
128 Long Acre, London WC2E 9AN

A Division of Pearson Professional Limited

First published in Great Britain 1996

© Pearson Professional Limited 1996

British Library Cataloguing in Publication Data
A CIP catalogue record for this book can be obtained
from the British Library.

ISBN 0 273 61708 7

1 3 5 7 9 10 8 6 4 2

Typeset by Northern Phototypesetting Co. Ltd, Bolton
Printed and bound in Great Britain by
Biddles Ltd, Guildford and King's Lynn

*The Publishers' policy is to use paper manufactured
from sustainable forests.*

THE AUTHOR

Sheila Cane is an expert at dealing with a diverse range of people and organizations in a career which has found her working with companies like Greenpeace, The Industrial Society, Virgin Group and The Institute of Management. Her main areas of interest include leadership, team building, stress management, service quality and individual coaching.

She is an experienced author and a regular contributor to TimeLife books on leadership and personal development issues.

THE EUROPE JAPAN CENTRE

The Europe Japan Centre is part of a major Japanese corporation, the Osaka Gas Group, with offices in Japan, the USA, Singapore and the UK. The Centre uses these international links to help its clients succeed on a global platform by offering them high quality research and human resources and management development expertise. Drawing on the staff's extensive personal experience of business practices around the world, the Centre offers a unique blend of *the best of East and West.*

THE BEST OF EAST AND WEST

The aim of the Europe Japan Centre is to be a major international influence in business.

To achieve this, we must be flexible, pro-active, informed and adaptable, and our core businesses of research, education and development should be delivered to our clients in a unique way by combining the best of East and West.

Our goal is always to be one step ahead, to anticipate the needs of our clients and to fulfil those needs to the very best of our ability.

We are committed to continuously improving everything we do, by developing our people and working together as a team.

CONTENTS

PREFACE TO THE SERIES

'Kaizen' offers something new to all organizations and to the people in and around those organizations: a philosophy and framework that encourages them continuously to set higher standards of performance and to achieve new goals in terms of customer satisfaction, sales and, ultimately, profit.

Kaizen is not a new concept. Literally, it simply means improvement, and many people when they hear it explained for the first time look relieved and say they have been doing it for years without knowing what it was called. This is not surprising; most people in the West, as well as in the East, have a desire to improve their work, their relationships, their lives, and many try hard to do so. But, in a management sense, improvement and Kaizen are not synonymous: Kaizen offers far more.

It is the intention of this series to explore exactly how Kaizen can offer more to organizations in the West, how it can help them pull step-by-step ahead of their competitors. In doing this, the Europe Japan Centre has unashamedly extended and modified the original Japanese concept of Kaizen, and has sought to combine the strengths of Western organizations with those of Japan. We are talking about Kaizen for the West, not about a slavish imitation of a concept 'not invented here'.

It seems to us that the time is right for this approach. In the increasingly competitive global market, companies are looking for ideas and practices that work, wherever they originate, not so that they can do exactly the same themselves, but so that they can adapt them to suit their own culture. At the same time, the recession in Japan and the questioning of many practices to which Japan's success has been attributed, means that Japan too is looking for new management ideas, and that for the West now to follow Japanese practices without adaptation would make no sense. Underlying the whole series, therefore, is our theme of 'the Best of East and West'.

Our approach to Kaizen focuses very clearly on the people element; each title is devoted to a group of people who are key to the success of an organization: leaders of the organization (*Kaizen Strategies for Successful Leadership*), the whole workforce (*Kaizen Strategies for Winning Through People*) and customers, be they internal or external (*Kaizen Strategies for Customer Care*).

For people who have looked on Kaizen principally as a set of processes for improving manufacturing, this approach may seem unusual. It is the experience of the Europe Japan Centre, however, that the most vital determinant in achieving lasting and continuous improvement is the attitude and behaviour of people, and that Kaizen strategies cannot work without the commitment of the people putting them into practice. Although most organizations may know this theoretically, their human resources practices, their leadership styles and their attitudes to customers by no means always reflect this knowledge. This series aims to help bridge this gap between theory and practice.

Researchers at the Europe Japan Centre draw on a worldwide network of contacts to locate and analyze the latest human resources and management ideas and trends. Our consultants and trainers combine these new thoughts with the Centre's practical experience in working with companies in the UK and continental Europe, so that our own services too are continuously improved. The awareness sessions, seminars, workshops and consultancy we offer are designed to help organizations of all sizes and types build on their strengths and create new, more effective strategies through their people. This series of books outlines some of our experiences, and brings together examples of the different approaches of organizations around the world.

The focus of the Europe Japan Centre and of these books is not, however, past practice or even current practice. What we are seeking to do is to stimulate thought, to concentrate the thinking of organizations on the future. Kaizen through people is one way of bringing the future closer, of inventing the future you want for your organization. We hope this series will help you do this in your own way, and we hope too that you will let us know of your success.

Chris Patrick
Director, Europe Japan Centre
July 1995

ACKNOWLEDGEMENTS

This book is the product of many people's minds and efforts. Each has contributed insight, facts, experience, introductions and personal support during its preparation. My contacts within companies around the world which have already embraced Kaizen have willingly given me time and access to information which has helped me understand and record in these pages the essential difference that a Kaizen approach to people can make.

I want to thank staff particularly at the Europe Japan Centre: Chris Patrick, Director, who read the draft manuscript and suggested many valuable improvements; Pat Wellington, whose experience of Kaizen and customer care provided many useful insights; Miranda Taylor, Researcher, who helped find and distil important sources of information; Tony Barnes, Peter Mieville, Justin Reay, Rachel Snee and John Banks, whose thoughts have made helpful contributions to various chapters; Sarah Bales for her work on training in Japanese companies; and Cristina Bevan and Dominique Kagawa who assisted in typing the manuscript.

My special thanks, too, go to Victoria Siddle at Pitman Publishing, whose support and enthusiasm buoyed me up through difficult times.

Sheila Cane
July 1995

INTRODUCTION

Why winning through people is important

'Our people are our most important asset'

How many times have we heard or seen these words? They appear in most annual reports, they are heard at meetings all around the globe, and they are never far from the lips of the leaders of the world's most influential organizations.

TRUE OR UNTRUE

And yet when the people who work in most of these organizations are questioned, they will tell you that in their perception the phrase is untrue because they do not feel that the organization (or the senior management) treats them as if they were of any real value at all. After all, in any time of financial hardship it is usually the Human Resource (HR) function that suffers the first cutbacks. Training is often regarded as a luxury that can be cut without any serious implications. Profit per employee has become a measure of how effective an organization is rather than any real measurement of the value and potential of each of the people employed. People appear to be expendable; any downturn in the market is followed by redundancies rather than an adaptation of the product or marketing strategy. HR senior managers may find themselves sitting on the board but rarely report that they feel themselves treated as of equal importance to other functions such as finance or marketing.

Why might it make sense to treat people as at least of equal importance as other assets in an organization? Any organization needs similar resources: adequate finance, appropriate technology, achievable plans and its workforce. No plan, however sophisticated, can be achieved unless the staff understand and are committed to it. No amount of investment can deliver success unless the staff are the best people to do what you want them to do. No amount of bright shiny leading-edge technology operates effectively without a positive interface with human beings.

People come first

So perhaps people *are* the most important ingredient to the recipe for success. People can be the raising agent – good, motivated and involved staff can make all other ingredients work together to provide the success that the organization has set as its goal. Poor, bored and mistrusting staff will make the other ingredients, however good, irrelevant.

Additionally, the rapid changes in the field of work in recent years have caused great concern to the workforce. No longer do they feel that they are secure working for a particular organization or even an industry, and therefore they tend to feel little loyalty to it. There is a tendency for people going to work to get what they can out of it, since that is the way they feel their employers treat them. There is a genuine sense of fear of change: people at all levels in an organization avoid it wherever possible. People talk about change and imply that they will embrace it, but the evidence is that there is much talk but little action.

Since any successful organization needs to respond and embrace change successfully and speedily in order to achieve its goals, it is vital to consider how to encourage the whole workforce to learn to live and work comfortably in the fast-changing world we now inhabit.

Some measurable signs that an organization has a workforce that is not likely to achieve its potential include:

- high levels of sickness
- poor time-keeping and high levels of absenteeism
- high turnover of staff
- unwillingness to accept responsibility
- unwillingness to embrace change (staff and management)
- poor quality standards
- high machine breakdown/accident figures
- low productivity in relation to competitors
- poor industrial relations
- low training budget in comparison with competitors
- obvious status levels – car parks, canteens, washrooms etc
- much downward communication – memos etc
- little upward and peer communication – suggestions, cross-departmental etc
- unachieved goals
- goals set at unchallengingly low levels
- high level of single skilled/single experience workers

How can an organization find a way to release the untapped potential of its workforce?

OBSERVING OTHERS

One of the ways an organization can learn valuable lessons for its future success through utilizing its workforce effectively is to explore different organizations' ways of working to discover what might be learned or adapted from their experience. In specific areas this may mean benchmaking. More broadly, however, it means looking around the world to find ideas, philosophies and practices that have worked well and considering whether they could act as springboards to new thinking.

The motor industry in both the UK and the USA in the 1970s was in an impossible situation, suffering from most of the list of danger signs above. In the UK, it was simply not able to build the number of cars planned, there was little investment available for new technology, and the quality of the work that was produced was low. In the USA, cars were extremely expensive to produce as productivity was also low and, as the market moved towards compact models, the major producers were still offering large, chrome, gas-guzzling monsters. By the 1990s the transformation has been staggering. The UK motor industry is now leaner, new technology is in place, industrial relations are transformed and productivity is soaring. The US motor industry has dramatically increased its productivity, models that customers want to buy are being produced and the major manufacturers are making healthy profits again.

How has this transformation been effected? By finding a new way of working with the workforce that allowed a turnaround in the situation

And where did they find their answers? In both cases the industry leaders looked to their most successful competition, Japanese companies, and either by entering partnerships, selling out or just borrowing the ideas, turned to the East for answers.

Many other industries were similarly looking to Japan to see if they could discover what the magic formula was that had enabled a major transformation since the end of the war, and had produced industries that were not only competing with but even out-performing the best that the West could provide.

PA Consultants, among many other organizations, arranged a study tour of Japan in 1987 and one of its members is quoted in the report as saying:

'... I would select two outstanding issues that left a marked impression on me personally *and these were the ways in which the*

Japanese enterprises harnessed employee resources to maximise contribution to the corporations, and it is this rather than technological leadership which gives them their leading edge. The second feature was the positive stance to survey and identify customer requirements rather than rely on uncontrolled feedback. ... the horizon as demonstrated in Japan is a long way off'

There were many parts to the answer they found. Firstly, the major Japanese companies had a much longer strategic view than Western organizations and once the strategy had been set, a human resources strategy was developed that became an integral part of the achievement of the overall strategy.

Secondly, because the intention of the human resources strategy was to cement the relationship between the workforce and the organization, a comprehensive communications structure, exhaustive training and delegation of responsibility seemed to be an integral part of the success.

Thirdly, a great deal of attention was given to attracting and employing the very best staff. Selection and recruitment involved many more people than was common in the West and took, in some cases, several months rather than hours.

Once the right staff had been employed, the induction process focused on the personal and human factors first, with job induction regarded as a continuous process.

To motivate staff, they were placed into teams with a good deal of autonomy about how they worked. They were appraised as a team, coached to improve performance and provided with skills training on an on-going basis. Personal development played an important role. Staff were encouraged to continue learning; even if what they were learning had no particular relevance to their work, it was seen as valuable in its own right and as encouraging people to become open to change and more flexible in their attitudes. Through the team structure, quality and continuous improvement were daily requirements for which each team was responsible.

Kaizen and its meaning

All these aspects of human resource management provide the vital human backdrop to a concept that the Japanese call 'Kaizen'. Kaizen literally means 'improvement'. As a management concept it was first made widely known to the public by Masaaki Imai in his book *'Kaizen: the Key to Japan's Competitive Success'* (1986). Western manufacturing companies were in some sectors quick to learn the process lessons from Kaizen; what some failed to consider and adapt sufficiently were the human aspects so closely related to the process changes. As a result, some companies failed and abandoned their attempts to change in this way; others made some progress but did not release the full potential of their workforce. Others have made great progress and are still engaged in the pursuit of continuous improvement.

This book is an explanation of part of a programme by the Europe Japan Centre to introduce the Kaizen approach to more organizations and through case studies to provide examples of how you might adapt it to meet your organization's needs.

It is important for Western organizations to realize that Kaizen is not something that can be picked at like an hors-d'oeuvres tray; it is an inter-related process that works as a whole, not as separate elements. It is also something that has to be adapted to make full use of the strengths of Western organizations. We, in the West, will need to take the principles of the process and readapt them to match the culture and conditions that we operate in.

Throughout this book, however, we will not be restricting ourselves to the practice of Japanese companies, nor suggesting that everything in the Japanese garden is rosy. The last three years have seen the emergence of economic problems in Japan, problems which have brought to the fore concerns about many aspects of social and working life. Just as the West looked to

Japan in the 1980s, Japan is looking again to the West for ideas – in areas such as human resources.

What this book aims to do therefore, is to identify the key human resource points which we feel have relevance in today's business climate and, more importantly, which may act as pointers towards future success. Rather than look to any single culture as a model, what we suggest is that organizations consider adapting the principles of Kaizen to achieve success by balancing the creativity of the individual (the best of the West) with the benefits of collective endeavour (the best of the East).

1

KAIZEN

改善

Although Kaizen is a Japanese concept, many organizations in the West have adopted its 'systematic common sense' with great success. Kaizen successfully utilized in the West is a combination of the best of traditional Japanese practice with the strengths of Western business practice by merging the benefits of teamwork with the creativity of the individual.

JAPANESE KAIZEN

Let's look first at Kaizen as it is practised in Japan, what is it and what does it involve?

Kaizen is in essence a very simple concept, formed from the two characters:

改

KAI meaning change and ZEN meaning good

thus together in one word they literally mean 'improvement'. Kaizen became part of Japanese management theory in the mid-1980s and management consultants in the West quickly took up the term using it to embrace a wide range of management practices which were regarded as primarily Japanese and which tended to make Japanese companies strong in the areas of continual improvement rather than innovation.

According to theory, the great strength of Japanese companies lies in their attention to processes rather than results. They concentrate the efforts of everyone in the organization on continually improving imperfection at every stage of the process. In the long term, the final result is more reliable, of better quality, more advanced, more attractive to customers and cheaper. Through Kaizen, therefore, the company will be able to produce better products or services at lower prices, and provide greater customer satisfaction.

HISTORY OF KAIZEN

Although the term 'Kaizen' first became apparent in the West in the mid-1980s, its roots lie in the aftermath of the Second World War. Following the defeat of Japan, the Americans were keen to encourage the nation to rebuild and, similarly to the Marshall Plan in Europe, General MacArthur approached several leading US experts to visit the country to advise them on how to proceed. One of these experts was Dr W. Edwards Deming who as a statistician with experience in census work came to Japan to set up a census. During his visit he observed some of the difficulties that the newly-emerging industries were under, and following his recent experience in reducing waste in US war manufacture began to offer advice. By the 1950s Dr Deming was a regular visitor to Japan and had built links with many Japanese manufacturers who were facing huge difficulties in terms of lack of investment funds, raw materials and components as well as suffering from low morale in the nation and therefore the workforce. By the 1970s many Japanese organizations had embraced Dr Deming's 14 key points for management. All of these have valid lessons for today, but I would pick out especially the following eight which have particular relevance to this volume:

1 The constant pursuit of purpose required for continual improvement of product and service.
2 A new philosophy to deal with change and customer needs.
3 Improving every process for planning, production and service.
4 Instituting on-going training on the job for all staff using a variety of methodologies.
5 Instituting leadership that is aimed at helping people do a better job.
6 Breaking down barriers that exist within departments and people.
7 Encouraging education for the self-improvement of every member of the organization.
8 Top management's commitment to improve all these points, specifically quality and leadership.

So the basis of thought that has led to a school of Japanese management techniques that have been envied the world over and thought of as particularly oriental, in fact originated in the US. It is strange to report that the US showed little interest in the work of Dr Deming between the war and the 1970s when Japanese exports began to make a marked impact. A prophet is often, indeed, without honour in his own land.

KAIZEN ATTITUDES

Most Japanese people are by nature, or by training, attentive to detail and they feel a strong obligation to be responsible for making everything run as smoothly as possible, whether it is in family life or at work. That is one reason why Kaizen works so well in Japan. However, in the West, this attitude may not be so consistent. The following examples illustrate the contrasting attitudes typical of both cultures:

'If it ain't broke, don't fix it.'

Western attitude: 'As long as you meet your targets, leave it alone, don't interfere.'

Kaizen attitude: 'Don't aim for perfection, it isn't good enough.'

'It's none of my business'

Western attitude: 'It's not my problem, I only work here.'
'It's not our department.'
'It's marketing's problem.'

Kaizen attitude: 'There seems to be a problem here, what can we do about it?'
'The production line has just made a great proposal to improve the design of the front panel.'

The swinging door: you walk past a cupboard door which keeps swinging open.

Western attitude: Ask someone to keep it closed.
Close it yourself.

Kaizen attitude: Look for the reason it keeps opening and remove the reason.

To encourage the Kaizen attitude within a Western organization requires a major change in corporate culture – to one that:

- admits problems
- encourages a collaborative attitude to solving them
- devolves responsibility to the most appropriate level
- promotes continuous training in skills and development of attitudes.

KAIZEN AND JAPANESE COMPANIES

The traditional Japanese approach to Kaizen embeds it in a hierarchical structure, although it gives considerable responsibility to employees within certain fixed boundaries. The key features of this management approach are:

- attention to process, rather than results
- cross-functional management
- use of quality circles and other tools to support continuous improvement.

Japanese organizations have so far been able to take a longer-term view of profit than their Western competitors because of their specific sources of financing. The Japanese tax system does not favour short-term investors and as a result, most organizations and their shareholders are focused on long-term success and profitability. Without the pressure of shareholders looking for regular short-term profits, they can take time and money to achieve market share and profit in the longer term.

They are also able to undertake long-term research and development and to examine and improve all the processes they are currently involved in. A Western company may focus all its efforts on producing a new product that will sell quickly; a Japanese company is likely to spend more time breaking down the process of production and making improvement continuously. Although individual improvements may be small, the cumulative effects can be impressive.

Japanese organizations tend to be strong in co-ordinating the activities of all their parts. Unlike Western organizations where barriers and competition between departments frequently lead to a lack of co-operation, the traditional Japanese training systems, lifetime employment and teamworking tend to make Japanese organizations more efficient in tapping the resources of all their people.

KAIZEN IN PRACTICE

The traditional Kaizen approach:

- analyzes every part of a process down to the smallest detail
- sees how every part of the process can be improved
- looks at how employees' actions, equipment and materials can be improved
- looks at ways of saving time and reducing waste.

The approach can be applied in many small ways by individuals going about their normal daily business. In an office, for example, that might mean asking questions such as:

1 Is the telephone in the most efficient place?
2 Are the materials placed so that I can reach them quickly and with little effort?
3 How can I save stationery?

If Kaizen is to be applied across an entire organization, however, teams will need to examine much larger issues.

In a workshop, for example, the questions might include:

1 How can we reduce wastage?
2 Is the equipment laid out so that we can use it efficiently in terms of time and movement?

3 How efficiently are supplies delivered and stored?

To enable companies to make tangible improvements, a whole range of tools have been developed. These include:

- Quality Control Circles, groups of people whose purpose is to continually improve quality
- process-orientated management, more attention given to the 'how' (the process) rather than simply the 'what' (the task)
- visible management, being seen, *'walking the job'*, being available
- cross-functional management, working across functional divides, to provide more unity and a wider vision
- just-in-time management (JIT), control of stock to avoid unnecessary expenditure
- kanban, a manual production-scheduling technique to control the flow of supplies
- statistical process control to enable each machine operator to control and measure quality
- PDCA: a process of Plan, Do, Check, Act to help solve problems.

Typically, all or most of these tools are used in the holistic Japanese approach to Kaizen. This is in contrast to the West, where some of these tools individually have been introduced as the 'answer' to every problem, without considering the context within which they were designed to work effectively.

KAIZEN IN THE WEST

Once Kaizen practices were identified as a key element in the success of large Japanese manufacturers such as Toyota, Western organizations, slowly, but surely, began to take an interest in the philosophy and practice of these companies. Particularly enticing to manufacturers suffering from Japanese competition were claims that Kaizen:

- leads to the reduction of waste
- can increase productivity by at least 30 per cent where no previous improvement process was in place
- is relatively cheap to introduce – it requires no major capital investment
- can lower the break-even point
- enables organizations to react quickly to market changes
- is appropriate in both slow- and fast-moving economies as well as growing or mature markets.

As we shall see later, UK companies such as Rover and Rolls Royce have adapted and implemented Kaizen practices with great success. But to what extent is Kaizen known outside the car sector in the UK? The findings of a survey carried out by the Europe Japan Centre in 1993* suggest a high degree of awareness among large companies.

Percentage of senior managers aware of Kaizen:

Large companies	94%
Small/medium size companies	44%

Actual experience of Kaizen, however, remains much more frequent in manufacturing than in service companies.

Percentage of senior managers in large companies with experience of Kaizen:

Manufacturing sector	88%
Service sector	53%

*Survey of Japanese Human Resource Practices in the UK, 1993

These figures suggest that although the pioneers were European subsidiaries of Japanese companies or other companies with a Japanese link (including Nissan, Sony and SP Tyres in the UK), a large number of other companies have recently started to follow the Kaizen route.

Interviews with senior managers in 50 of the leading 250 UK companies suggest that Kaizen is viewed as a positive influence. The most frequently cited views included:

- it is an extremely powerful concept that has a great deal to offer
- it is an essential ingredient for future competitiveness
- it leads to higher quality goods and services
- it can lead to a more efficient organization
- it improves business results
- it helps eliminate waste.

Although the majority of the reactions were positive, the survey also identified several areas of concern among companies which had implemented Kaizen. Three main points emerged:

1 It is difficult to achieve Kaizen in practise, because it requires a complete change in attitude and culture, and needs the energy and commitment of all employees. It also requires a substantial investment of time.
2 It is difficult to maintain enthusiasm for several reasons:
   - some people see Kaizen as a threat to their jobs;
   - a lot of poor ideas tend to be put forward as well as good ones, which can be demotivating;
   - by implication, there is never complete satisfaction.
3 Continuous improvement is not sufficient on its own, major innovations are also needed. There is a danger of becoming evolutionary rather than revolutionary.

Sometimes it may be better in the long term to improve the way things are done, but it may not make commercial sense in the short or medium term.

None of the concerns are reasons for not introducing Kaizen, as with thought and planning all of them can be overcome or mitigated, as we shall see, but managers need to be aware of them and spend time thinking about them, rather than abandoning Kaizen before it has a chance to yield positive results.

From the point of view of employees and unions another fear often voiced about Kaizen and Japanese practices in general is the fear that people might improve themselves out of a job or be asked to do more work for no additional rewards.

In Japan the previous commitment to lifetime employment tended to remove these fears, but in the UK the commitment may understandably be less. Companies such as Rover, influenced by their co-operation with Honda, have made employment commitments to their workforce. It is also essential for management to stress the positive benefits of Kaizen for the whole company, showing how improvements in quality and productivity should lead to the growth of the business in other directions. Senior managers should also consider how the benefits of Kaizen can be passed on in the form of financial or other rewards.

Initial considerations

Although some Western companies have taken 'continuous improvement' to mean merely the introduction of sophisticated suggestion schemes to bring continued and long-term results, the introduction of Kaizen involves considerably more sweeping changes in attitudes, structures and processes. If it is not to be considered only as the latest management idea – here today and gone tomorrow – senior management need to think about the impact and implications of Kaizen, as well as about the practicalities of introduction. In particular:

- senior management commitment is essential
- senior managers must be aware of Kaizen's role in the overall business strategy
- all employees should understand Kaizen's role in their work
- Kaizen should be linked to personal development and enablement.

In Japan, the cultural background means that senior management commitment can be taken for granted. Local guidelines therefore concentrate on the shopfloor involvement. In the UK, where the cultural background is different, ensuring the right management commitment is essential.

Senior managers need to understand Kaizen and how it fits into the organization's overall business strategy. They should also be aware of the implications and potential disruptions that the introduction of Kaizen might bring:

- reorganization of people into teams takes time and may be disruptive
- training and group meetings take additional time
- productivity may decline temporarily while changes are implemented
- some employees may be suspicious and unco-operative.

Above all senior managers must be prepared to let go of some areas of power: Kaizen in practice is based on the belief that the people doing a particular job will often know better than anyone else (including their supervisors) how that job can be improved, and that they should be given the responsibility for making those improvements. Management needs to be prepared – mentally as well as practically – for this shift.

KAIZEN v. INNOVATION

Kaizen's step-by-step approach is in direct contrast to the great leaps forward in innovation.

Managers in the West should not be so enthusiastic about Kaizen that they neglect the wider issues of planning for major growth by innovation as well as gradual improvement. The introduction of Kaizen should free senior managers to think about the long-term future of the organization, look for new opportunities and concentrate on strategic issues. Kaizen will support the improvement of existing activities, but will not provide the impetus for the great leap forward. It is vital to retain the balance between innovation and improvement.

AN APPROACH FOR THE WEST

As the desire for cultural change sweeps through Western companies, whatever their size, Kaizen can be seen as one way of effectively achieving that change. Although we have so far stressed the attitudinal or qualitative changes involved, an equally important part of Kaizen is its quantitative element. It is only by combining measurement with attitudinal change that Kaizen can be effective. The diagram below represents in a simple schematic format the main points involved in creating a Kaizen-based organization in the West:

	Aims	Hows	Whats
Frontline	CHANGE	IDEAS	MEASURE
Tactical	LEADERSHIP	TEAMWORK	ROLES
Strategic	MISSION	REWARDS	STRUCTURE

Soft ◄————————————————————► Hard

It is the role of strategic 'management' to be responsible for the implementation of an effective mission, (purpose) reward and organizational structure. It is the responsibility of tactical and strategic managers to exhibit and practice sound leadership, promote good teamworking and ensure that people understand their roles. It is also the responsibility of everybody in the organization, from the front-line through to the board, to measure themselves and their team, to identify in quantitative terms areas for improvement, to generate ideas to change practice and procedures and measure again to ensure this improvement has been achieved.

Each time a process or service is measured, it can be analyzed, areas for improvement found and implemented, and a new standard achieved and measured. The cycle then continues through further analysis and improvements as shown in the diagram below.

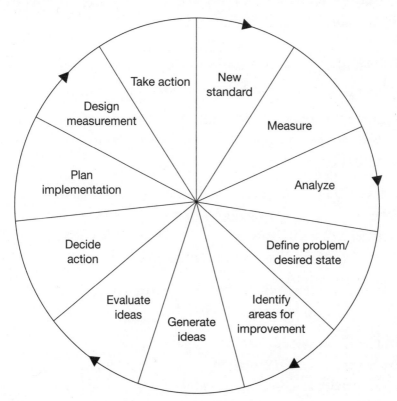

In a company which wants to adopt Kaizen principles, it is everybody's responsibility to be involved in this cycle of improvement. Everyone must therefore be given the knowledge, skills and tools to participate fully, not only within their own team, but also within cross-functional teams and across the organization as a whole.

A frequent difficulty encountered when organizations begin to introduce Kaizen in the West is that many employees lack the confidence to take on greater responsibility or to make decisions for themselves. In addition to training in skills, tools and knowledge, it is therefore vital to ensure that the right climate for change is established.

Core values

The core values of a Kaizen programme which everyone in an organization needs to aspire to are:

Trust and respect for every individual and the organizational belief that:

- each individual should value and respect every other individual, not just people in their own department, their own specialisation, or their own level

- every individual should be able to openly admit any mistakes he/she made or any failings that exist in his/her job, and try to do a better job the next time. Progress is impossible without the ability to admit mistakes.

It is out of these values that the Kaizen culture develops and creates 'Kaizen' people, who exhibit:

- attention to detail
- forward-looking approach
- receptivity to constructive advice

- willingness to take responsibility
- pride in his or her work and organization
- a willingness to co-operate.

The introduction of Kaizen has now spread well beyond companies related to Japanese companies, as Dutton Engineering illustrates.

HOW EUROPEAN COMPONENTS ADAPTED KAIZEN

A classic example of adaption of the principles of Kaizen rather than just a complete adoption is that of European Components, a subsidiary of the Japanese Takata Corporation, which manufactures automotive components on two sites in Belfast, Northern Ireland. The automotive components market is increasingly a global marketplace with manufacturers sourcing from whichever supplier can offer the highest quality, lowest cost and best delivery – no matter where they are based.

European Components' overall business objective is to be number one in car seatbelts in Europe, a goal which sets them against considerable competition from suppliers in terms of cost, price and delivery. The company took a fundamental decision that no Kaizen tools and techniques were to be used for any process unless they supported this objective.

To achieve this, a number of five-year targets were set:

- 30 per cent market share
- zero defects in all activities
- factory costs to equal 75 per cent of sales
- improved internal and external communication.

The company then used an approach they termed 'policy deployment' to turn its overall business objectives into meaningful departmental targets. Each department's responsibilities were established in relation to the overall target.

Departments were set one-year targets with monthly assessments for each of them. Although it was easy to measure many of

▶

the targets, some of the departmental activities proved more difficult. Some of the cost-cutting activities undertaken by the personnel department to support the overall target of factory costs equivalent to 75 per cent of sales included:

- tying in elements of the training plan to saving costs
- flattening the organizational structure by taking out layers of management
- reducing monthly canteen costs
- improving absence levels
- evaluating departmental budgets and overtime
- reviewing the company magazine.

Detailed improvements are specified on monthly assessment forms for each item and training is introduced to help people meet these objectives. Any problems in performance are detailed in a monthly meeting of all managers.

European Components believe that there are a number of factors crucial to the success of Kaizen in their company.

Planning

Planning is essential to identify the activities that need to be improved. They believe that Japanese managers spend up to 80 per cent of their time planning, while European managers spend up to 80 per cent of their time acting.

Good housekeeping

This ensures a safe, pleasant and efficient working environment. It also provides a good first impression for new customers visiting the plant.

Leadership

Kaizen gives a focus to everything in the company, so it is important that senior managers are committed to its success.

Patience

Kaizen is not a quick fix. It is hundreds or thousands of small changes, so it is important that people do not expect too much, too soon.

HOW DUTTON ENGINEERING ADAPTED KAIZEN

Dutton Engineering (Woodside) Ltd, currently based at Sandy in Bedfordshire, UK, is a subcontract sheet metal working company and after a management buyout in 1993 is owned by its Chairman and Managing Director. Its strategy in the 1980s was towards Quality and to go for BS5750/2 so Ken Lewis, the Managing Director, decided to visit Japan to explore future quality standards for his company. What he saw inspired him. 'I realized' he says 'that there was nothing the Japanese were doing that we couldn't do in the UK. However they were doing something that, at that time, in the UK we were not – the Japanese trusted the people who worked for them, the people trusted the management, and their companies trusted their customers and suppliers.'

Returning to Britain, he put everyone into teams on the same salary regardless of education and experience and when he introduced a system of annual hours, the teams began to see the advantages of working together. Once the tasks were completed, the team could go home and 'they worked a lot more efficiently when they realized that', he says.

Duttons has worked hard to build trust relationships with the staff, suppliers and customers. 'Our people now spend time in customers' plants, learning more about their needs, finding out

▶

▶ how we can serve them better. After all, we want our customers to be successful. It's vital to break down barriers and recognize that we all want the same thing.'

The results are impressive, between 1991 and 1994:

The turnover per month of direct employees (non-administrative) rose from £5,000 to £7,500.

The value of work in progress and stock fell from £276,000 to £113,000.

In 1994 Duttons won the DTI Wedgwood Trophy for its pursuit of excellence.

Ken Lewis identifies Duttons success as based on:

- leadership of senior management giving the organization a vision and having confidence that it will take you there
- trust and value of the staff
- trust and good relationships with suppliers and customers
- managers identifying and developing people's skills
- preparing thoroughly before the introduction
- identifying any 'terrorists' (managers who might sabotage) and involving or eliminating them
- 'work smarter, not harder'.

CHECKLIST SUMMARY

The Europe Japan Centre believes Kaizen in the West has the potential to combine the best of traditional Japanese practice with the strengths of Western creativity and enablement. The best way to implement this successfully is:

1 Consider, research and plan which aspects of Kaizen can be adapted to work for your organization.

2 Build Kaizen as an integral part of your business strategy.

3 Get the commitment of senior management.

4 Balance the benefits of teamwork with the creativity of the individual.

5 Consider any difficulties that may occur and plan how to resolve them.

6 Finally, remember that Kaizen is an on-going process. Continually review, improve and adjust the implementation in line with your vision.

2

LINKING
BUSINESS
STRATEGY
AND
HR STRATEGY

O nly organizations that place as much priority on their human resource strategy as their business strategy will have the strengths to become or remain first class.

The first step to winning through people with Kaizen is to give a higher priority to human resources than ever before. Most business strategies in the West have failed because they have ignored the vital component to winning – the workforce. How can organizations reverse this trend by setting up people-based strategies which can cope with the rapidly changing demands of the global marketplace?

In Japan it has long been the case that business success has been as much based on the management of people as the management of technology. Although some of the ideas used in Japan originally came from the West, Japanese companies adapted them in a uniquely effective way, acknowledging in reality the theory of the importance of the workforce. The Japanese method of people management is in some ways inimical to many Western people and indeed is now being questioned in Japan, but the goals of developing people – and the underlying attitudes of trust and respect – are worth serious consideration.

There is no single right way, no panacea to solve human resource issues. What works in one organization may be quite inappropriate for another. Two key points should, however, be borne in mind:

改

1 Strategic business goals should never be considered without linking them with human resource strategies.
2 Whatever your business, if you have the right people you will succeed.

An effective human resource strategy will enable you to find and develop these people, the 'right' people, the best people.

It is almost a cliché that, in many organizations,
people are a wasted resource.

It is an essential part of management's role to prevent this waste of human resources, encourage the development of people and set up new, less hierarchical structures to allow people to grow. Many managers talk about 'empowerment', but very few genuinely put it into practice. Large scale rethinking needs to take place before people can be developed to take more responsibility and to make the contributions that they are capable of. A major part of this rethinking involves the issues at the heart of a human resource strategy.

- how to motivate people
- how to reward people
- how to educate people
- how to develop people.

A business strategy can only be achieved if the people
responsible for delivering it are committed to it and
trained to perform well.

Too many companies fail to maximize their potential because they consider their business strategy in isolation. It is therefore essential that an organization's overall strategy is linked from the very beginning to its human resource strategy. The two strategies should operate hand-in-hand, so that any modifications or developments in one strategy are reflected in the other.

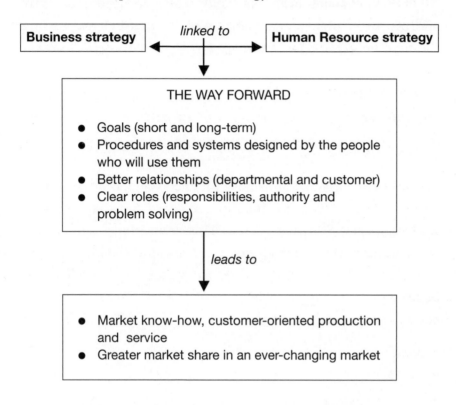

HR STRATEGY OF THE FUTURE

Three key changes will drive business and human resource strategies for the future:

1 As the practice of de-layering continues and organizations flatten, there will be fewer traditional opportunities for promotion up the hierarchical ladder.
2 The quickening pace of market change means organizations will need to respond even more rapidly to take advantage of new opportunities.
3 Business opportunities will occur in a wider range of geo-

graphical and product service areas and information gathering activities will need to be wide-ranging and prompt.

All of these changes mean that senior managers need to urgently address the challenge of organizing new structures and finding the right people for the future.

As standardization of products and services increases people are often the only point of difference between competing organizations

---

Traditionally, organizations have planned the people they need in terms of jobs. For example, in five years' time we will need 200 engineers, 50 drivers, etc... This is no longer sufficient – skills are important, but so are attitudes and behaviour.

The requirements for the workforce of the future are likely to be far wider and far more demanding than in the past. Employees will increasingly need to be:

- creative
- flexible
- multiskilled
- co-operative (good team players)
- confident
- knowledgeable about the business
- customer orientated
- quality orientated

Any human resource strategy for the future must address the question 'What sort of people will our organization need?' Once this question is answered, a strategy to meet these needs can be established.

Who should set the human resource strategy?

In Japanese organizations the personnel department is held in higher esteem than many other departments. For this reason those who wish to progress into a key strategic function will often be happy to work initially in personnel.

Too often in the West the personnel/HR department creates a human resource strategy in isolation from the rest of the organization. In some cases, the human resource strategy is of little interest to the board, and the personnel department is not treated with the respect human resources deserve.

If a company is seriously interested in becoming a Kaizen-based company the senior management team will show its commitment by involving itself in setting up the human resource strategy, even if it is only discussing the principles and demonstrating commitment, whilst leaving the details to others.

The human resource department can play a vital role in enrolling senior management in the understanding that the overall business plan can only be achieved through employees. Using the commitment of senior managers to their business strategy, it is possible to gain their genuine commitment to a positive human resource strategy. One method of doing this is to consider to what extent previous strategic goals were reached and what differences an effective human resources strategy might have had to 'sell in' the idea internally. Quoting as many examples as possible of organizations benefiting from the sort of strategy you are encouraging can also be persuasive, if senior management is reluctant to place sufficient emphasis on HR considerations.

If a genuine commitment is not achieved at senior level, the chances are that success will evade the organization and, yet again, expectations will have been raised that are then unfulfilled.

A number of organizations are now using cross-functional working groups to finalize the details of their HR strategy. Some are also involving people of various levels of experience, length of service and backgrounds to ensure that the strategy reflects a broad perspective and is relevant to the needs of the workforce as well as the longer-term needs of the company.

COLGATE-PALMOLIVE

Colgate-Palmolive Co. has a clear vision for its future 'To become the best truly global consumer-products company'. To ensure that Colgate attracts and retains those with the skills and interests to pursue international careers, it set up a global human resources strategy team, comprising senior line managers and senior HR leaders to work in partnership with management to build organizational excellence. The year-long development process produced:

- a set of international values that emphasize care for Colgate people, consumers, shareholders and business partners;
- an order for all employees to work as part of a global team
- a commitment to continuous improvement
- strategies for generating, reinforcing and sustaining organizational excellence (including recruitment, training, compensation and recognition systems).

The global human resources strategic team's work was unveiled at a week-long global HR conference attended by the Chairman, the President and Chief Operating Officer, each division's president and more than 200 of Colgate's HR leaders representing 35 countries.

Strategic planning is not simply the preserve of large organizations. It is just as important for medium and small organizations to involve their staff in business and HR planning. A feasible method for organizations committed to improvement is to set up a series of workshops, with voluntary participation, to discuss issues such as:

- what do we want to be able to say about ourselves?
- what do we want our customers to say about us?
- what do we want our suppliers to say about us?
- what do we want our industry to say about us?
- what do we want our neighbours (the local community) to say about us?

Out of these workshops a vision for the future should emerge, which can provide the foundation for business and HR strategies.

Some organizations have gone further in involving people in their strategies.

The Vanguard School (a non-profit organization in the US) hosted a mission statement workshop and invited:

- current, former and potential future students and parents
- teachers and school administrators
- members of the board of trustees
- college recruiters
- former, current and prospective donors.

In the UK, the **Austin Rover Group** recently reshaped its strategic vision, again by involving a range of internal and external stakeholders.

Such organizations recognize the importance of all stakeholders (interested parties) and the benefits of involving them in helping to create their future direction.

改

HR STRATEGIES TO WIN THROUGH PEOPLE

An HR strategy document may take many different forms. While it may include overall aims for personal development, it may also be useful explicitly to cover a number of specific personnel practices.

Six areas that are worth considering by organizations seeking to achieve the goal of winning through people using Kaizen are:

1 A recruitment and selection policy that involves all employees.
2 An induction programme that involves corporate, departmental, team and individual members.
3 An on-going education and development programme that encourages all employees to become multi-skilled and helps them to reach their full potential.
4 An appraisal system that develops people and increases co-operation between them.
5 A reward system that is motivating and non-divisive.
6 A never ending programme of continual improvement (Kaizen) which improves every area of work and involves everyone.

(See later chapters for a detailed discussion of each of these elements.)

If a strategy is to succeed, everyone should know about it.

Once the human resource strategy is created as part of the overall business strategy and commitment is in place from senior managers, the next stage is to communicate it throughout the organization. By their very nature, these strategies may be either detailed or very broad in outline but they are rarely inspiring to read. For inspiration and motivation, other documents and practices are necessary. One of these may be a mission statement or purpose.

THE ROLE OF A 'MISSION' STATEMENT

A major trend among organizations wishing to involve their staff fully has, in recent years, been the use of 'mission' statements, although this title may not always be used. 'Corporate statement', 'statement of objectives/goals' or, increasingly popular in the UK, 'statement of purpose' are all in common use.

Whatever the name, the statement should unify the purpose of the organization with its values, behaviour standards and strategy.

THE MISSION STATEMENT

It therefore will contain the broad outlines of both the overall business objectives and the human resource strategy that has been so carefully thought through. Most importantly it should mention employees as a key part of the 'mission'.

Some examples worth considering are:

ICL:

We will achieve our mission by providing challenge and opportunity for our employees, releasing their skills and creativity.

Royal Dutch/Shell Group of companies issue a small booklet entitled 'Statement of General Business Principles' setting out their business objectives followed by their responsibilities to four groups of people (their stakeholders):

- Shareholders
- Employees
- Customers
- Society

The section on responsibilities to employees reads as follows:

'To provide all employees with good and safe conditions of work, good and competitive terms and conditions of service; to promote the development and best use of human talent and equal opportunity employment; and to encourage the involvement of employees in the planning and direction of their work, and in the application of these principles within their company. It is recognised that commercial success depends on the full commitment of all employees.'

Hewlett Packard produce a three page policy statement that sets out the company's purpose and an explanation of Management by Wandering Around and Open Door Policy that they believe is a fundamental strength of the company's success. Page Two and Three are worth reproducing in full as they are both inspiring and set standards to which the employees can relate. A classic case of 'this is what we want from you and this is what we can give you in return.'

HP WAY – BUSINESS RELATED

1 Pay As You Go – No Long-Term Borrowing
- helps maintain a stable financial environment during depressed business periods

- serves as an excellent self-regulating mechanism for HP managers.

2 Market Expansion and Leadership based on New Product Development

- engineering excellence determines market recognition of our new products
- novel new product ideas and implementations serve as the basis for expansion of existing markets or diversification into new markets.

3 Customer Satisfaction Second to None

- we only sell what has been thoroughly designed, tested and specified
- our products have lasting value – they are highly reliable (quality) and our customers discover additional benefits while using them
- best after-sales service and support in the industry.

4 Honesty and Integrity In All Matters

- no tolerance for dishonest dealings with vendors of customers (eg bribes, kickbacks)
- open and honest communication with employees and stockholders alike. Conservative financial reporting.

HP WAY – PEOPLE RELATED

1 Belief in Our People
- confidence in, and respect for, our people as opposed to depending upon extensive rules, procedures, etc
- depend on people to do their job right (individual freedom) without constant directives
- opportunity for meaningful participation (job dignity).

2 Emphasis on Working Together and Sharing Rewards (Teamwork and Partnership)
- share responsibilities: help each other; learn from each other; chance to make mistakes
- recognition based on contribution to results – sense of achievement and self-esteem
- profit sharing; stock purchase plan; retirement programme; etc,

▶

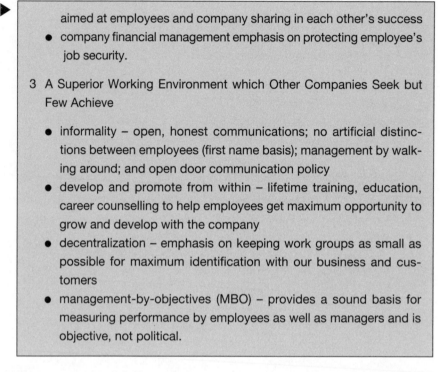

aimed at employees and company sharing in each other's success
- company financial management emphasis on protecting employee's job security.

3 A Superior Working Environment which Other Companies Seek but Few Achieve

- informality – open, honest communications; no artificial distinctions between employees (first name basis); management by walking around; and open door communication policy
- develop and promote from within – lifetime training, education, career counselling to help employees get maximum opportunity to grow and develop with the company
- decentralization – emphasis on keeping work groups as small as possible for maximum identification with our business and customers
- management-by-objectives (MBO) – provides a sound basis for measuring performance by employees as well as managers and is objective, not political.

A common pitfall with mission statements is that nobody remembers them or takes them seriously. Various methods can be used to get over this. The mission statement, for example, could be printed in a clear form and given to each member of staff as well as being clearly displayed on notice boards, etc. A good example is Braitrim PLC, one of the UK's largest suppliers of plastics and packaging, who decided to print their mission statement on a sealed plastic card and give it to every member of staff. It is also printed on the back of every visiting card (therefore ensuring that suppliers and customers see it).

Another method of ensuring staff remember the 'mission' is to involve them in developing it, and later in improving/changing it.

In larger organizations, it may also be worth setting up working groups to implement the mission statement at different levels and with as much work as possible devolved to those people directly involved.

BRAITRIM

Our Purpose

We at the Braitrim Group are committed to being a world leader in our chosen activities.

We will encourage and support the continuous improvement and well-being of our people.

By anticipating our customers' needs and surpassing their expectations, through excellence of service, product innovation and care of the environment, we will sustain the long-term business partnerships that will assure our future.

It is important to remember too that any strategy and statement of purpose will need to be reviewed regularly to ensure that it remains appropriate to the conditions in which the organization is operating and that it can be continuously improved. Kaizen should be operated on the mission statement and other strategy documents just as much as on processes and services.

改

CHECKLIST SUMMARY

- An HR strategy planned in a vacuum will never be as constructive and productive as one developed in direct relation to the business strategy. (And vice versa!)

- The HR strategy should be the blueprint by which the organization's operational directors can transform the corporate development vision into a practical reality.

- This means acknowledging the importance of the Personnel Department by crediting it with the same operational (or line) status as, say, Production rather than, as usual, seeing it as a backwater, staff function; in other words, the Personnel/HR function should serve the business's market-building goals as equally as it serves employees.

- Involving the Personnel/HR function in strategic planning should come about through cross-functional collaboration.

- This will enable the Personnel/HR Department to derive a coherent and co-ordinated people strategy that rolls forward – that is, keeps in step with – the changing needs of a rolling business plan.

- Any strategy will amount to no more than an idea unless it is communicated, and legitimized by senior management committing to it unequivocally.

- The legitimization can be expressed through what is variously called a mission statement, a values statement, a roles and goals statement, a corporate statement or a statement of purpose.

- Communicating the statement should be universal: all trading stakeholders (employees, customers and suppliers) must know the organization's purpose (its ends), and its strategy (its means).

3

COMMUNICATION

As the previous chapter indicated, the first step to gaining the workforce's commitment to a change in strategy is through communication. Good communication is also a key link in the operation of Kaizen in any organization and may prove to be a minefield unless particular care to get it right is taken early in the process.

Communication is, by definition, the means by which ideas and information are transferred and therefore effective communication exists when the transfer is clear and the recipient understands the message exactly as it was sent. It is implied that this is a two-way process and that it is just as important to listen as to speak. Any means to improve the effectiveness of an organization's communication will pay huge dividends. Effective communication is based on equality and respect between the parties communicating to ensure clear reception. It is interesting to remember here that one of the two core human values for the operation of Kaizen is:

Trust and respect for every individual.

If a company wants to operate Kaizen successfully, it needs to review its communications systematically. Within the organization itself, as much importance needs to be attached to the smooth functioning of upwards and cross-functional communication as to traditional downwards communication.

Communication within the company

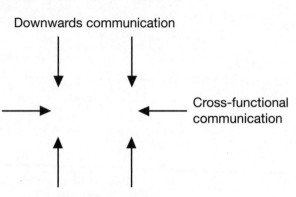

Downwards communication

Cross-functional communication

Upwards communication

The organization's communications with related parties outside (suppliers, shareholders, customers, etc) also need to be subject to scrutiny and improvement.

Communications outside the company

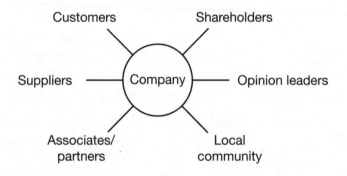

Customers

Shareholders

Suppliers — Company — Opinion leaders

Associates/ partners

Local community

IN-COMPANY COMMUNICATION

When any business goes through a major change, a clear, consistent integral communications strategy is vital to explain the positive benefits of the change. Internal communications are one of the most important elements of the communications mix. Staff briefings, information packs, magazines and publications all have a part to play in building understanding.

The very best form of effective communication is usually face-to-face meetings and there are key influences within any organization – management groups, workteams and key employees – who can form the focus of the 'marketing' campaign. These key influences can help to develop a communication channel through the organization to spread important messages.

HOW EFFECTIVE IS ORGANIZATIONAL COMMUNICATION?

Generally speaking, organizations do not devote enough effort to considering how effective their communications are, and how they could be improved.

The easiest way of finding out how employees perceive the effectiveness of the organization's communication is to ask them. But a word of warning: you may not like what they have to tell you. Before taking on a project, the Europe Japan Centre always interviews employees throughout an organization to gauge its culture and effectiveness, and the results, almost without exception, reveal difficulties in communication and lack of involvement. Common responses include people thinking they need:

- to know more clearly where the organization is going
- to know what other people in the organization are thinking
- to feel the 'them and us' is disappearing
- to know where they personally are going (career development)
- to be involved in discussions before decisions are made ('we hear most things by chance', 'senior managers don't always tell managers things, sometimes we find out first').

The grapevine in an organization is often the most effective form of communication ('if you want to know anything around here, ask the tea lady') and considering how many times it is the bearer of bad tidings, management would benefit enormously from making sure that the message that is going around is the correct one. One confectionery manufacturer in the UK has recognized the truth of this and called one of its weekly newsletters 'The Grapevine'.

In this area as in other HR areas, cosmetic surveys are counterproductive. Before asking for feedback, it is vital that management are prepared to act on that feedback, or at least explain why they cannot or will not. Asking people what they want and then not giving it to them without a good reason is usually even more upsetting than not being asked in the first place. Raised and then dashed expectations are highly demotivating.

Two companies who did ask their employees for feedback and were prepared to take action to satisfy the criticisms are Anglia Water and British Airways.

ANGLIA WATER EMPLOYEE SURVEY

Anglia Water, a new privatized utility company, commissioned an external research organization to design a questionnaire which was distributed through the internal mail systems but returns were made anonymously to the external company. (Many employees are keen to voice their opinions but find anonymity helpful to overcome any concern that they will be victimized.) The results were then published in a special edition of the staff newspaper to demonstrate that the results were being taken seriously and also to give employees an opportunity to judge their views in relation to the majority. Some positive things were said about salaries and benefits, the company's approach to training, health and safety as well as quality. But performance-related pay and the management style which one respondent described as 'management by fear' came in for strong criticism. The company launched a follow-up programme to involve staff in helping to resolve the problems identified as well as building on the strengths uncovered by the survey.

Anglia Water considers that although anonymity was important to at least getting genuine responses, it is the follow-up programme that is gaining the commitment and respect of the staff.

BRITISH AIRWAYS EMPLOYEE SURVEY

British Airways also launched a major employee survey called 'Input 93', to which nearly half of its workforce responded. The results were that the majority wanted:

- a better understanding of the business
- greater recognition of a job well done
- better communications
- improved working conditions
- flexible working opportunities.

British Airways has responded by a complete overhaul of their current performance management systems so that individual performance is now matched and measured against that of the team within which the individual works. It has also acknowledged the need to build a more participative management style which involves individuals more closely in the business. The HR department has set up a long-term project to resolve these issues.

Both these surveys, and there are many more with similar results, show that, in general, workforces want more information, more responsibility and to know what it is that they need in order to contribute more to the organization.

How has communication broken down?

What has typically gone wrong? How has the West so often drifted into a breakdown of trust and communication between management and its workforce?

Although some problems are deeply embedded in social and

economic structures, the more recent roots lie again in the aftermath of the Second World War. The US and UK looked to the successes of their armed forces for their management styles, while the Japanese had, as it were, a clean slate with which to proceed to get the very best out of what few resources they had. This resulted in the US and UK believing that:

- people will do what they're told
- people will do what they are paid for
- people cause failures
- failure means disaster, and someone must take the blame,

while broadly, the Japanese moved towards believing that:

- about 98 per cent of people want to do what is right
- most people, if given ownership of a problem, will help solve it
- people can correct the problem by improving the system
- failure always represents an opportunity for improvement.

The US and UK belief system led to a top-down imposition of standards and the brains of their employees being left at the factory gate, except when they were used against the management, and an atmosphere in which the gathering in of the mass of traditional knowledge was seen as 'expropriation'. In short, an alienated workforce.

It is clear that where communication breaks down, there can be little workforce commitment to an organization's goals.

What we are looking for in the West is a balance between a control of the processes and the commitment of the people. And this can only be built through communication between the two sides in order to build a relationship of trust and unity.

Everything an organization does sends a message

Communication is not simply writing memos or speaking to staff, it is everything an organization says and does. One aspect of this that the Japanese have understood and where they provide a shining example is the area of status.

Every manager who has a company car, a reserved parking space, a separate office, a special canteen or key to the executive washroom is sending a message to their staff. 'My work is not the same as yours, mine is more important.' This immediately down-grades the value of the employee and is unlikely to achieve involvement or motivation.

This issue of the relative importance of different people in an organization can cause great difficulty. The senior management of a major London hotel were battling with the concept that possibly the cleaners were at least as important as they were, until they realized that if one of them were ill not very much changed (at least in the short term) but if one of the cleaners were ill, it caused a serious problem and someone else had to be found to do their work.

Unless staff are convinced that their work is regarded as being important, they are unlikely to do it particularly well. And most of the time, it is lower salaried staff who are actually producing the goods or serving the customers which is where the profits are produced. It is important, therefore, to reduce the visible status symbols that your organization uses to reward senior staff, and at the same time to communicate, verbally and through processes and structures, the importance of the contribution of all staff.

NEW UNITED MOTOR MANUFACTURING

New United Motor Manufacturing Inc. (a joint venture between Toyota and General Motors) in Fremont, California has found that practices such as open offices, a single parking lot, a common cafeteria, uniforms and athletic and social activities both inside and outside the plant have served to reinforce the new democratic

▶

structure and atmosphere of common goals and win-win consensus they were seeking. This is a far cry from the anarchy that existed at the plant when General Motors closed it down in 1982. Using 85 per cent of the same workforce, the Japanese-style management turned the plant around in two years to achieve international recognition for its world-class quality and productivity in a climate of harmonious labour relations.

SEMCO

At Semco, one of Latin America's fastest growing companies, getting rid of executive dining-rooms and other 'democratic' policies, including parking on a strictly first-come-first-served basis, are seen as part of running a 'natural business'. As Ricardo Semler explains: 'At Semco we have stripped away the unnecessary perks and privileges that feed the ego but hurt the balance sheet and distract everyone from the crucial corporate tasks of making, selling, billing and collecting.'*

*'*Maverick!*' by Ricardo Semler (Arrow Business Books 1993)

WALKING THE TALK
(or putting what you say into action)

In a Kaizen organization, managers and the team leaders are visible and easily accessible to the staff they work with. It is difficult for people to respect someone who earns considerably more money than they do, when they cannot see what they are doing or understand why they are doing it. If a manager is in daily contact with his team, seeing what they are doing and asking their opinions, it is much more likely that a relationship has a chance to develop.

If an organization wants its workforce to be 'enabled', it will not help simply to tell them that they are! People need to feel for themselves that they are becoming powerful and that takes action from the management to create the conditions where it can be realized by the staff themselves.

It is all too easy for the 'lip service' empowerment syndrome to become a source of amusement for staff if:

- decision making remains with management
- employees are only allowed to recommend not implement
- employees are not given freedom to decide **what** to do, (only how to do it)
- managers still see the problem as how to motivate staff
- jobs are allowed to remain repetitive and unsatisfying.

The personal approach is also important at key moments in any organization's development. If the Managing Director has a message for the whole staff, it is often much more effective to deliver it in person at a large meeting rather than expect it to filter through the management tiers unadulterated. Memos and videos have a role to play, particularly in larger organizations, but remember that they also carry the hidden message that the Managing Director does not think the workforce valuable enough to spare the time to speak to them directly.

How far do you go?

The extent to which senior managers should disclose financial or strategic information to all employees is a major issue for many organizations undergoing cultural change. If people are to contribute fully to helping an organization succeed, they clearly need to be well-informed, and increasingly this means having information about the financial and market position of their organization. Although traditionally management have been reluctant to divulge many details in these areas, sometimes through fear of the information leaking to competitors and sometimes from the fear that it may lead to higher wage demands, in practice there appear to be few cases of these behaviours, providing the organization is operating overall in a manner perceived as fair and open by its staff.

In organizations where employees are owners, the disclosure of financial information is inevitable (see Chapter 11). In other organizations, it has frequently had beneficial results. At Levi Strauss in Blue Ridge, Georgia, for example a quality enhancement programme was installed accompanied by profit sharing, with excellent results.

LEVI STRAUSS

In an evaluation survey six months into the programme, employees responded overwhelmingly that they understood the concept and measures, thought they were fair and could affect them. The company also considered that one of the obstacles to implementing the programme at other Levi plants was the reluctance of some departments to disclose information as required.

Source: *'Competitive Advantage Through People'* Jeffrey Pfeffer, (HBS Press 1994)

SEMCO

At Semco in Brazil, managers decided to share information about their financial performance with all their employees. Although at first some managers were alarmed, and did not want their salaries to be disclosed, the majority went ahead and made the information about themselves available. Other information was also disclosed, and with the union's help, a course set up to help people understand balance sheets and cash flow statements. These measures are considered a vital ingredient to involving the whole workforce.

These strategies are not limited to large companies. A small chain of restaurants in the South-West of England has told the Europe Japan Centre that they decided to open their books to their employees, initally at a time when employees were asking for a pay rise and could not believe there was no money to fund an increase. When they had seen the financial results, and established there was no extra money available, the employees not only dropped their pay claim but became avid cost-cutters themselves. Once enlisted and trusted in this way as full partners in the enterprise, attitudes changed remarkably quickly, and led to increased profits the following quarter.

UPWARDS COMMUNICATION

Kaizen places great emphasis on upwards communication: ideas from people on the shopfloor serving customers or in other 'front-line' positions need to be able to work their way up the organization and contribute to the overall performance improvement of the company. In Matsushita (manufacturers of Panasonic and Technics products), for example, 25,000 implemented changes climb up through the hierarchy every year.

How can an organization improve communication upwards? One method which lies at the heart of Kaizen is suggestion systems. At best these have enormous benefits to a company, including greater participation by staff, a greater sense of involvement, increased motivation, interest, responsibility, recognition, and reward. In addition they can help both to tap and release further aspects of people's potential. The system (of which there are many variations) can apply individually or as part of small group activities, often in Quality Circles (QC) and Total Quality Control (TQC) programmes. Surprisingly perhaps, the original motive for introducing the idea was, apparently, not merely economic but to boost morale and develop staff. Nevertheless it has developed into a very effective way of improving working methods and conditions with huge savings for many companies, along with direct improvements in productivity and, most significantly, 'Quality'. Perhaps no other single aspect of Kaizen is more widespread and successful. It is crucially important that those people most affected by change have input in (and responsibility for) the nature of that change.

Suggestion systems operate in all sectors, from large manufacturing companies like Toyota to banks such as Sanwa. The numbers of suggestions from staff can be in the 1000s per annum and the procedures for processing them vary and are often sophisticated. In all cases they produce significant results.

Like other Kaizen features the use of a suggestion system is by no means exclusive to Japanese practices, many companies elsewhere having adopted and developed their own methods. Indeed it seems that the first systems in Japan were introduced shortly after the Second World War, and Training Within Industry (TWI), soon followed by the 'revolutions in quality' partly instigated by Deming, Duran and others.

One of the key apparent differences between the Japanese practice and those subjects adopted elsewhere is their readiness to incorporate the suggestion system into a longer-term policy, and not use it merely for short-term results or on an *ad hoc* basis. In addition, their criteria for evaluation are not based merely on immediate cost saving. This is fundamental, and mirrors the whole Japanese philosophy and approach to Human Resources and company policy generally. According to Kenjiro Yamada, Managing Director of the Japan Human Relations Association, the suggestion system should go through three stages:

1 Encourage suggestions, however simple, to help improve the job and workshop. This will help people to look at the way they are doing their jobs.

2 Emphasize employee education so that people can provide better suggestions. In order to do this they need to be equipped to analyze problems and must be educated to do so.
3 Following increased education the economic impact of suggestions (from both a company and the individual point of view) should then be introduced, but only after the first two have been properly established, with the increased interest that they inspire.

A problem in the West has been that companies have tended to go straight to the third phase, without the first two and without the morale-boosting participatory spin-offs. As a result, they have tended to be less successful. It is evident that training and education form the basis for their effective introduction.

The purpose for the operation and remit of suggestion schemes needs careful preparation and integration within company policy. One key issue is that of personal reward. Small rewards, with high participation rates can have greater economic impact than higher rewards and lower participation rates. Some companies prefer no reward. Once again the methods need careful planning before implementation.

A flow chart of a scheme in use by a successful UK company is shown on the following page.

CROSS-FUNCTIONAL COMMUNICATION

Implicit in Kaizen is the practice of inter-departmental (or cross-functional) co-operation. In simple terms this means that there should be a readiness to work with other teams or departments in the areas of the transfer of skills, ideas and information. This will also facilitate quality implementation into the whole process of product delivery or service. Too often, it seems, there is a failure of communication between groups which have an

改

WINNING IDEAS

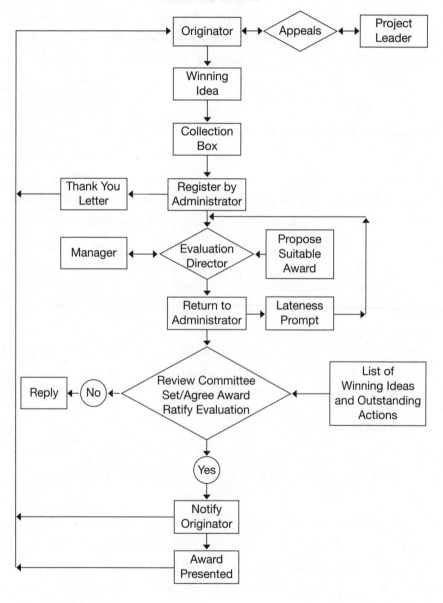

equally important role in the company's activities. There is good reason to think that members of any one link can provide valuable insights for the benefit of others. For example design engineers could gain invaluable information from sales and marketing people about customer behaviour and requirements; production engineers could provide practical help for design engineers into the realities of the production process; line workers important information on production systems.

This cross-functional work should not be *ad hoc*. The appropriate interaction of different stages should be part of policy and company strategy, with time allocation for such co-operation. This interaction between functions will add to company cohesion, and does not imply a blurring of job definition; if anything it helps to clarify more precisely the area where there is no overlap.

One of the quickest and most effective ways of improving performance within most organizations is the introduction or improvement of inter-departmental communications. Internal barriers protecting mini-empires are common even in relatively small companies. Not only do these barriers cause friction, in many cases they can cause inefficiency – a typical example is duplication of work – and, worse still, customer dissatisfaction, when, for example, the sales department promises delivery of a product which the production department knows it cannot manufacture in time.

Cross-functional teams (*See* Chapter 6) help to break down barriers, and are vital in a Kaizen organization, but a whole range of other measures from the formal to the informal can also pay huge dividends.

Organizations with canteen and leisure areas, for example, find that many problems are solved by informal discussion over a cup of coffee rather than lengthy meetings set up formally. Hewlett Packard have coffee stations at regular intervals in their buildings and encouage staff to meet to chat through projects for just this sort of informal creative problem solving. Other organizations have thriving social programmes, sports events, quizzes etc which bring people from different departments together.

On a more formal level, the benefits of short-term job rotation and shadowing are becoming increasingly clear. In a company where the Europe Japan Centre worked recently, we brought together people from the accounts department and sales staff. Feelings had been running high as the sales people blamed the accounts department for producing the paperwork they needed too slowly, while the accounts people saw the sales staff as an unwelcome distraction to their main work. Only by bringing the two sides together in an atmosphere of non-blame, was it possible to air the problems fully, for each side to understand the other's problems, and for everyone to find effective means of working better together. It became clear, for example, that paperwork could be decreased, that the sales department could reduce pressure at the end of the month when the accounts department was busiest, and that the accounts department could simplify the data they needed from sales.

Office or factory lay-out can also play a major role in breaking down barriers. One of the reasons why product development has been so successful in the Japanese electronics industry, for example, is that designers and researchers have worked physically closely to the shopfloor. At Semco in Brazil 'the purchasing and engineering department have been scrambled together so that everyone sits together, near the factory. The idea is that we all can learn from each other.'

In-company communication should of course include part-time, as well as full-time, staff. As the proportion of part-time employees increases, an organization will only succeed if it is able to tap the creativity of these employees too.

The Japanese retail sector provides several good examples of companies which have realized the importance of part-time employees.

SHIMAMURA INC., JAPAN

Shimamura Inc. is a type of discount store company with 266 branches across Japan; it sells mostly women's clothing and household items.

It is different from many traditional companies in its human resources programme, which:

1 Allows part-time employees the opportunity to take high positions in the company.
2 Encourages active participation of all employees, whether full or part-time.

Unusually for Japan, half of all the shop managers are women.

Part-time employees

The company has the philosophy that basically part- and full-time employees are equal. They enjoy the same rates of pay, the same benefits and the same promotion opportunities.

The reasons for this policy are that the company feels many women would be extremely good employees but cannot work full-time, so their abilities are wasted. The shops are also sometimes in areas where it is difficult to get staff; part-timers can solve this problem. The company prefers to employ local staff, not specifically because of costs, but because they feel local staff understand local customers best.

Kaizen

The company has a series of five manuals which all employees in the stores must know and use: these contain all the information necessary for employees and they are encouraged to make pro-

▶

posals to improve what is in the manuals (and therefore the way the stores operate).

Once a suggestion is made, there is a strict procedure for dealing with them. Suggestions considered good by the shop managers and senior executives are announced at the monthly meeting held for shop managers. The employee(s) who suggested it is rewarded, and notices about the suggestion and person(s) are displayed on notice boards.

Keeping momentum going

The company is very conscious that suggestion schemes often lose momentum. Therefore:

- All suggestions are reacted to within a month.
- Good ones are incorporated in the manuals immediately, so people can see progress occurring all the time.
- Those which are not used are returned to the person who suggested them, along with comments.

As a result between 500 and 800 suggestions are made each month.

NEW ERA COMMUNICATIONS

New technology and changing business practices are creating major new challenges for organizations in terms of communicating with their employees. A rapidly growing number of companies are battling with the problems of communicating not only across different locations in their own country, but also in locations around the world. At the same time, technology is allowing more and more people to work at home, some, most or all of the time, with the need to devise new ways of keeping them in touch with developments.

At present as many as 10 per cent of British companies employ people who work from their homes, according to the Government's Employment Gazette. British Telecom estimate that by the end of 1996, 2.25 million people will be working from home for at least three days a week, while SW2000, business forecasters, say the figure will rise to 5 million by the end of the century. In the USA, Link Resources estimate that around 5 per cent or up to 7 million of the USA workforce telework. Teleworking exists too in organizations of all sizes, from one to two people operations who would formerly have rented High-Street offices and commuted, to SMEs and major organizations. At Digital in the UK, for example, around 1,000 of the 4,000 staff no longer work in a conventional office-based way. In the USA, IBM allows teleworking on an informal basis, with about 2,000 of its 10,500 staff working from terminals at home and encouraged to come to the office only twice a week.

While statistical studies have identified clear benefits from teleworking in terms of reduced costs and higher productivity (people who work from home are up to 20 per cent more productive than those in the office, according to BT), disadvantages focus on communications and related problems.

Drawbacks of teleworking

Hard to manage	45%
Social isolation	32%
Communications difficulties	32%
Lose touch	19%
Unavailability for meetings	16%

* based on the opinions of employers with the potential to employ teleworkers

Source: *Independent*, 18th July 1995

If organizations want to benefit fully from the advantages of teleworking, they need to give serious consideration to these drawbacks, and invest time and energy in ensuring they do not lose the vital creative and social talents of their people. Regular phone contact with other teamworkers and home-workers, as well as with the office, is vital, and so is the opportunity for face-to-face contact.

Other techniques include:

- team meetings
- socials
- gossip boards
- E – mail
- video links.

Whatever communication problems organizations may face within their country of origin, it is certain they will be intensified in a global operation. Although new technology offers tremendous potential for making improvements internationally – companies can draw, for example, on the particular expertise of people in different countries and can communicate with them 24 hours a day – it is extremely important that cultural differences are recognized in setting up those communications channels.

Between the UK and Japan, the Europe Japan Centre has experience of many breakdowns in communication within branches of the same company. Typically areas of misunderstanding include:

- different attitudes to deadlines
- different approaches to quality
- failure to transfer sufficient background information about a request or project
- communication with the wrong person
- lack of understanding of the overall aims of the company.

Cultural training can help raise awareness of the general issues, but care should always be taken to be clearer and more explicit in communications (and to write down the most vital issues) than in one-country situations.

Training to improve communication

It may be that staff need more information before they can begin to communicate. Often they do not contribute to a debate because they do not know who to talk to. Does everyone in your organization know what people do and what they are responsible for? It may be that they need additional training in business and financial reporting to even understand the organization's Annual Report. Senior management may feel that they are communicating by issuing a copy of the report to each member of staff but this is of no value unless it can be understood. Organizations who run Employee Share Option Programmes have found this sort of training invaluable (*See* Chapter 11).

It is also worth considering training on computers, E-mail and the Internet to ensure that all members of staff have the ability to communicate within as well as outside the organization. There are still many techno-phobes who are unable to communicate or find information as effectively as they might because they are frightened of new machinery. Many organizations are now based in different buildings and cities (if not countries) and electronic mail is now becoming a necessity if the organization is to work effectively as a whole.

Organizations may wish to consider enrolling all staff (including management) in effective communication-skills training. Everyone thinks they know how to speak and how to listen when the evidence is that each and every one of us could improve – and this book is about continuous improvement in order to release the untapped potential of people in the organization.

改

Meetings

So much of an organization's communication takes place in meetings that it is worth considering how they can be made more effective.

How often have we heard the following:

'Meetings, bloody meetings, that's all I do'

'There are too many of them, they last too long and don't seem to be about anything'

'Meetings are just an excuse for my boss to bore us all into submission'

'We talk about things but nothing ever gets followed up, nothing ever happens as a result'.

The purpose of a Kaizen group meeting is:

- to target areas for improvement
- to constantly upgrade people's awareness of problems and how to solve them through team effort
- improve communication
- to break down barriers
- to cross-fertilize ideas
- to foster individual and collective improvement
- to enhance individual team and company performance.

Meetings therefore have a valuable role to play in an organization's effective communication, and to get the best out of them, the tried and tested ideas for improvement are worth recalling:

- have a clear stated agenda for every meeting
- limit each meeting to a particular time
- elect or nominate a chair and notetaker for each meeting
- make sure everyone present needs to be there and that they know *why* they are present

- make sure no one individual speaks too much
- spend at least a few minutes at the end ensuring everyone knows what has been agreed and compiling action plans
- review the meeting process to see how it can be continuously improved.

The meeting process includes the following:

- making sure that any assessment is open and understood
- encouraging team identity and respect for individual differences
- encouraging originality and creativity.

Meeting evaluations might include the following to be rated 0–5:
- was everyone informed in advance
- was everyone fully prepared for their role
- was everyone committed to dealing with common issues
- was the room comfortable and well-equipped
- did it start on time
- was there a clear, well presented agenda
- was the agenda followed efficiently with flexibility
- was there concentration on one issue at a time
- were issues properly considered before moving on
- was there good co-ordinated listening/speaking interaction
- did everyone contribute actively
- did everyone clearly present their genuine feelings and ideas
- did everyone respond constructively to others' input
- was there spontaneous creative energy and thought-stimulated openness.

One process that has proved to be successful to encourage the more reticent in meetings to contribute more and to control those who find it hard to stop talking, has developed from the women's movement. When the meeting has been opened and everyone is clear about the topic and purpose, suggest that any speaker can only make a limited number of contributions and that each contribution can only last for a limited period of time. This can lead to much more clarity of contributions and clear debate and is well worth considering.

It is the role of the chair of the meeting to ensure that everyone makes their contribution and this will require some tact and the use of open questions. We have all attended meetings where we have been asked 'You all agree, don't you?' and seen individuals with a valid point unable to respond.

PINBOARDING

Another useful technique, especially for quite a large meeting, is 'Pinboarding', developed by Bennett Consultancy Services. It enables groups to reach effective decisions quickly, ensures full participation and therefore builds 'ownership' of the decision ensuring commitment. Simply, it involves stating the rules at the opening: all ideas are recorded on individual cards or post-it notes, no one talks for longer than 30 seconds. At the end of the meeting, the cards can be photocopied giving an accurate, complete and immediate set of minutes.

HOW A UK FOOD COMPANY USED COMMUNICATION TO TURN AROUND

The company

A UK food manufacturer, founded over 100 years ago, employing 120 staff with a turnover of £10M, until recently in family ownership but now part of a large group.

The problem:

Although the company regularly returned a profit, in the early 1990s the management identified several key areas of concern which together meant it was ill-equipped to cope with the challenges of the next few years:

- static financial performance
- pedestrian in terms of innovation
- unprepared for more stringent food safety requirements
- poorly placed to beat more powerful competition
- customer service below required standard
- not very good industrial relations with many petty grievances
- hierarchical and autocratic management.

The process of change – Stage One

Management made the decision that if the company was to survive and prosper, attention had to be focused on two areas:

- Investment in the facility.
- 'Turning the people around' and involving them in the business.

This case study focuses on the second of these priorities.

From the start, the new management made the decision that they had to break down the 'them and us' culture; they wanted to introduce a new culture of confidence, open government and involvement. They decided to do this gradually, but systematically.

Their first steps included:

- *an open door policy*: managers made themselves widely available to all employees, regularly spent time on the shop floor, committed themselves to giving as many direct answers as possible, gave out more information about the business to all employees etc. As a result, people in different positions in the company began to understand more about the business, more about other people's problems and skills, and more about their own role in the business.

- *bringing people together from various departments to resolve issues*; rather than launching straight into a team approach to

▶

everything, *ad hoc* groups were set up on specific issues and answers worked out for some of the major problems, for example on quality and supply. In this way, people began to see the value of working together in groups to solve problems, and some of the barriers that existed between different departments began to be removed.

- *skills training*: new skills, particularly computer training, had been neglected, so staff were now encouraged to volunteer for training. As a growing number of staff became more proficient in using the computer, other – more fearful – members of staff were encouraged to volunteer for it, so that finally very few people remained computer illiterate. (Note: which incidentally also gave them access to even more information)

The process of change – Stage Two

As the climate in the company began to change, management decided to move the programme into its next stage: much greater management involvement of all employees. This included a number of major steps:

- instigating regular company meetings. The company is small enough for everyone to gather together in one large room, so twice-yearly meetings were introduced at which the senior managers spoke about the company's past and present performance and staff were encouraged to ask questions. Initial criticisms were that there was too much management talking, the meetings too short and the information too statistical – all aspects that were resolved in later meetings.
- introducing team working.
- introducing a Kaizen programme.

At this stage the Europe Japan Centre was invited to help the organization and to reinforce management's determination to introduce change. They interviewed a cross-section of people throughout the company to establish areas of strength and concern before devising a programme spread over several months to allow implementation of new techniques and ideas between sessions.

- running two hour-awareness workshops to help the whole workforce understand the changes going on in the company and to gain their support and enthusiasm
- running discussion groups with senior management on maintaining the momentum for cultural change and half-day workshops to develop a mission statement and cultural vision
- leading seminars and workshops to assist in the introduction of Kaizen
- leading workshops to improve the performance of team leaders and help create real teams, rather than work groups.

By the end of the programme, many positive changes had been brought about:

- team meetings of 20 minutes per week within work time are allowed for discussion
- business knowledge has increased: daily sales figures are posted on the notice boards; the annual sales plan is available for any interested employee to take away and read
- the team building and quality programme are going well
- multi-skilling and cross-functional working are showing positive results.

The results

- appreciably higher output
- £100,000 saving on the direct labour budget
- a 30 per cent increase in service levels

Less immediately tangible, but nonetheless important, results include:

- a happier, more committed and more responsible workforce

改

- closer relationships with and higher standards from suppliers
- an atmosphere of continuous improvement
- a greater dedication to quality and customer care.

Although this particular company agrees that it still has a considerable way to go to achieve all it set out to and then even when it gets there, there will still be further to go, it is easy to see that so much of what has been achieved has been due to effective communication. Each step has involved meetings, discussions, workshops and responding positively to queries and criticism.

It is also heartening to observe that the organization has taken the spirit of Kaizen to its soul, acknowledging that nothing is ever perfect but that the purpose is that pursuit on a daily and yearly basis.

善

CHECKLIST SUMMARY

- Communication is the key link in every Kaizen organization.

- All Kaizen organizations operate with the understanding that every individual has a major part to play within the organization. Every single person in the company must have a full 'picture' of what their company's aims are.

- Communication has to be twofold! Managers must 'listen' and act upon relevant information.

- Blame is about fear – fear of losing one's job, making oneself feel foolish. The Kaizen approach is to get the message across that 'failure' means there is room for *improvement*.

- All staff, regardless of their position in an organization, must be made to feel that they are contributing to the 'whole' and that their contribution is important.

- Staff who are not in touch with the final 'customer' must be informed about what part they play in the 'whole' process and encouraged to understand that they too are contributing to the customer's satisfaction.

- Managers and team leaders must be seen 'on the job', available to staff who need their advice, on a daily basis. They must also encourage staff, at whatever level, and show appreciation.

- All staff should feel free to make suggestions for improvement of their own work areas, and how they can help the next stage (department) in the overall process without fear of retribution.

- Cross-functional management, or inter-department co-operation, is the essence of a full understanding of a company's aims.

- Training, education and communication for *all* staff is paramount to a Kaizen approach.

4

RECRUITMENT
AND
INDUCTION

Consider the type of people you need to make your organization challenging and innovative, not just the jobs you need to fill

An organization may well have a human resource strategy full of statements about employing the best people and listing the values and qualities they will require, but how are they to find them when vacancies arise?

PREPARING A RECRUITMENT PROFILE

Too often, at present, the previous occupier of the post is described and a clone sought to replace them. This is likely to maintain the status quo rather than promote organizational development. The principle of continuous improvement embedded in Kaizen suggests a new approach. Rather than aiming to replace the individual with a mirror-image, it is valuable to consider what sort of person you would require if all the conditions of the HR strategy were involved.

If your HR strategy states that you want the very best staff, what would 'best' mean in this position?

1 What skills, competencies and experience would they have?

改

2 What personal characteristics would they show?

In Chapter 2, the likely requirements for the workforce of the future were identified as:

- creative
- flexible
- multiskilled
- co-operative (good team player)
- confident
- knowledgeable about the business
- customer orientated
- quality orientated.

Using this list as a prompt, consider which are the most important to this particular position and how you will be able to judge them. For example, if an application says they are a good team player, what questions will you ask them to be able to assess for yourself the likelihood of them fitting into your team?

The Europe Japan Centre takes the premise that virtually anyone is capable of developing Kaizen attitudes, and if the organization is committed to operating and developing them, then they certainly will in time develop a Kaizen approach, but by selecting people who already have Kaizen attitudes the process can be accelerated.

The more an organization can prepare a profile of both the skills and experience required balanced with the personality and qualities required, the more likely it is that a good match can be found. It is also more likely that a creative input to the team can be found that is in line with equal opportunity employment. In the past, female, young, older and applicants from a different ethnic origin found themselves restricted by conditions of education, experience or age categories when they might have been perfect for the role, and even today many of these attitudes die hard.

In a team role, it is worth considering what additional

qualities might be required to lift the entire team performance. Many teams do not recognize that someone slightly different to themselves might be the perfect catalyst for them all. It is always much easier to employ someone 'just like us' rather than take the bold step of employing someone different and enjoying the challenge they will pose. The HR department may find that counselling the department with a vacancy to help them consider employing a catalyst will pay dividends.

SEMCO

At Semco, employees are fully involved in the process of recruitment. First of all, no single person can decide that a job opening exists; although an executive can suggest the need for a new person, the whole business unit needs to agree, before a profile can be put together and the job advertised. The profile includes the qualities and requirements, such as experience, leadership experience, languages spoken, and gives a weighting to each. Academic background and personal appearance are excluded as a matter of policy.

The first step in recruiting is always to put the profile on the in-company bulletin boards, so that internal applicants get the first opportunity. Under a programme known as 'The Family Silverware', Semco chooses an employee who meets 70 per cent of the job requirements, under the assumption that this person will be able to develop quickly the additional 30 per cent necessary. Before anyone is hired (and indeed promoted) however, everyone in the unit has the opportunity to interview and evaluate the candidates.

Source: 'Maverick' by Ricardo Semler (Arrow 1994)

RECRUITMENT ADVERTISING

Too often at present, vacancy advertisements are largely based on the job title and salary printed in large letters, with a middle paragraph containing the qualifications and experience required in small type-face. This approach has proved to have drawbacks:

- titles rarely give a genuine picture of what the job involves
- by emphasizing salary the advertisement may attract people who want to work primarily for money
- qualifications gained some years ago and experience of present equipment and processes are rarely good criteria for satisfying the requirements of the future.

The costs of employing the wrong people are very high. The disruption to the department and the team of a new person leaving almost immediately because they did not understand what the job was really going to be like are added to all the costs involved in another recruitment.

Innovative organizations around the world are rethinking their advertising for new recruits and the application forms they use emphasize the sort of values and qualities they require. It is worth considering what your current recruitment advertising says about your organization. If the advertising is fairly conventional, but one of the stated aims in your mission statement is to be innovative, you are sending a mixed message and unlikely to attract the 'right' people for your future success.

Avid Technology, a film-editing system maker in Massachusetts, US, with 320 employees and a turnover of $50 million, screens potential recruits on its ten core values, including teamwork, honesty and passion to win.

The **Body Shop** based in Sussex, UK, has devised a questionnaire for all potential franchise holders which includes questions such as 'How would you most like to die?'

INTERVIEWS

Once an organization has received a batch of high-quality applications and created a short list of what it believes are the most likely, how should it go about interviewing them?

Firstly, it is important to have clear criteria as to what is required in the position and this should be discussed before the vacancy is advertised. Interviewing should be based on these criteria.

> One major Hotel in Las Vegas has found a novel way of shortlisting potential recruits. It insists that all candidates fill in their application forms in the office, where they are met by HR executives who shake their hands before deciding whether to give them a form or not. The HR department believe that if an applicant is happy to shake hands and look a stranger in the eye under stressful conditions, they are the right sort of person to be considered for a post in their hotel. If not, they are thanked for attending and turned away.

Currently most selection interviewing is a fairly brief affair with both sides on their very best behaviour. Often only two or three people will interview an applicant and they are very unlikely to be potential colleagues of the applicant. The interview process very rarely takes longer than two or three meetings, each lasting less than one hour, and many organizations are proud to be able to complete the process within one day.

Time is, of course, a valuable resource but employing a new member of staff is a very important process and perhaps deserves more time and attention. Many Japanese companies both in Japan and overseas, have very different policies.

> **Toyota, UK**, for instance, tell prospective employees that they want 'the right people for our company' and potential recruits have to go through the following process:

▶

- four to five hours testing and orientation
- four to five hours at an assessment centre
- one 45 minutes final interview
- a one-and-a-half hour medical.

Toshiba, UK aim to recruit staff as objectively as possible and to ensure that the applicant has an opportunity to gain a broader perspective of the organization. It does this by:

- showing two videos to ensure they clearly understand the organization and its aims
- giving each applicant three separate interviews with managers from different departments
- holding at least one interview with a manager from an area which the applicant is not trying to join.

It may appear to a Western organization that this example is excessive but it is worth considering that the majority of middle-sized US organizations who have won *Inc.* Magazine's Employers of the Year awards quote a 'rigorous recruitment process' as one of the foundations of their success. This might include five or six interviews, some with the team in which they will be working, and even up to half a day spent with an industrial psychologist.

MOS BURGER

A Japanese fast food chain operating on a franchise basis places a strong emphasis on franchisees who share the company's values and philosophy. The company competes directly with the burger giants such as McDonald's, but sees its strength in people. The recruitment process is therefore stringent.

- each applicant has to pay a nominal fee for the company brochure and information
- after reading the company information, prospects are invited for an in-depth discussion on the reasons why they want to join the group
- if they still want to run an outlet, they have to visit ten group outlets, interview each owner and write a report on their impressions
- they then visit a number of competitors and do the same
- those who still want to join are interviewed several times, first by an area director, and then if successful by senior management.

The group feel that this process is necessary to ensure that they are sufficiently motivated and that their attitudes are in line with the company.

The lesson seems to be that if an organization genuinely wants the best people, it will need to invest more care (and probably more time and attention) in how to attract and then select its potential recruits.

INDUCTION

Having selected the new recruits how then should an organization introduce them into its ranks?

Induction is the indispensable first step to creating lasting commitment

In the past, induction has consisted of that terrible first day when the personnel manager takes the recruit's references and medical certificates and shows them their desk.

It is well worth remembering that particularly in a time of high levels of unemployment, it is likely that the new recruit may be feeling very nervous; they might even have left a secure job. They need to be impressed with their new organization or they will leave. If they are skilled, experienced and exciting enough for you to want to employ them, it is likely that other people will want them as well.

The main aim of an induction programme is to encourage a positive way of thinking in your new members of staff.

Traditional induction programmes are treated as a means of giving information to new members of the organization, or as a way of integrating people so that they become a productive part of the workforce as quickly as possible.

In an increasingly competitive global marketplace, this may not be enough. Organizations need people who not only share their goals but are committed to furthering them. Induction is an ideal way to start a new way of thinking in an organization. New people are generally enthusiastic (if nervous), open-minded and full of goodwill towards their new employers. It is an ideal opportunity to build on these feelings to achieve benefits throughout the organization.

It is worth considering what messages the organization's current induction programme gives in relation to its stated core values. Many are in conflict with each other, as demonstrated here.

STATED CORE VALUE	INDUCTION ACTIVITY
• We think long term	• Half day programme
• Staff are self-movitated	• Endless lectures
• We are innovative	• Boring introductory lectures
• We care about our staff	• Throwing staff in at the deep end

---

The right first impression is crucial, not only for the future of the individual but for the future of the organization.

Sales and marketing know the importance of a first impression; it can make the difference between an easy sale or a hard sale, or even no sale at all. It is important to treat employees in the same way, to make sure that their first impression is a good one.

- how many organizations give equal consideration to the thoughts and feelings of new employees as they do to their customers?
- how many managers realize how crucial it is to give the right first impression?
- a poor induction programme can leave a lasting impression of inefficiency and lack of concern that can take months to eradicate.

The benefits of a good induction programme are considerable:

- a positive start creates goodwill and positive feelings
- high commitment is encouraged. People who start off being committed are more likely to remain committed
- lower staff turnover, fewer grievances and reduced absenteeism are likely to result
- long-term savings on recruitment and training costs are possible
- higher measurable productivity can be achieved.

A good induction programme includes giving the new employee the 'bigger picture', letting them know what the organization is all about and where it wants to go. Nobody wants simply to be a cog in a wheel but too many induction programmes are designed to create even more cogs. The classic management fable demonstrates this perfectly. A man walked down a road to find three people doing things with bricks creating different levels of height; he asked each in turn what they were doing. The first said 'I am cementing one brick on top of the other', the second said 'I a building a wall', while the third said proudly, 'I am building a cathedral.'

Organizations are increasingly realizing that to be successful in the long term, all members of staff need to be involved in the 'bigger picture'. It is therefore vital to tell them:

- the mission of the organization
- its philosophy
- where it is going.

Japanese organizations have focused on this approach for many years. Information about the organization, rather than about the jobs, formed the core of the induction programme. Typically new recruits would learn about the following topics during their first week:

Mission	Goals
History	Philosophy
Structure	Communications
Products	Services
Current market position	Planned market position
Customers	Competitors

The induction programme also places particular emphasis on ways of working and attitudes to work. From the outset, traditional Japanese programmes stress the following characteristics:

1 Quality – Ensuring that all members of staff develop an appreciation of the importance of total quality in all aspects of their work, including customer service.
2 Teamworking – Nissan UK, for example, state 'we believe in teamworking wherein we encourage and value the contribu-

tion of all individuals who are working together towards a common goal'.

Only after new members of staff have a clear idea of the company, does training for the job begin. From the outset, all new recruits have a clear idea of why they are doing a specific job and how it fits into the bigger picture. This has a number of benefits:

- it adds value to the job
- the new recruit feels more responsible and highly-valued.

Traditional priorities for induction programmes focus on three main areas:

1 Job information – Why the job is done, how it relates to other work, performance standards and measurement of standards.
2 Company information – Products and services, structure, communications and reporting relationships.
3 Personal information – Working hours, holidays, renumeration, facilities and special conditions.

There are a number of reasons why these priorities need to be reconsidered:

- people work best when they are free from stress
- events and circumstances in private life can have a considerable effect on working behaviour
- in many cases, it may be more effective to deal with personal matters first
- induction can then move to company information and the bigger picture before moving to job information.

It is worth considering whether the whole induction programme places enough importance on the person. People want to know what will happen to them in the company, what will be expected of them and what they can expect from other people.

改

Many organizations have now reversed the traditional pattern and moved towards:

1 Personal Information – Expanded to cover personal and career development, attitudes and expectations.
2 Organization Information – Expanded to include mission, goals and the bigger picture.
3 Job Information – Expanded to focus on the processes involved (eg quality and teamwork).

All members of staff are valuable, yet many are not reaching their full potential

Induction for all staff

Too often, induction is regarded as a must only for graduates or recruits at a certain job level. Increasingly though, organizations are realizing that all members of staff are important and that many are not reaching their full potential because they lack the information or motivation to do so. Certain UK companies have taken the decision to formally induct all members of staff from senior management through production to administration staff, where all staff are given a common core of information about the company and its goals, before specific job training begins.

The director of a UK printing company, while on a trip to Tokyo, was early for an appointment and spent some time talking through an interpreter to the receptionist of the small Japanese company he was visiting. He was amazed at the amount he discovered from this receptionist about the company's products and sales and was so impressed by the good impression it made on him as a potential customer that, on his return to the UK, he immediately instituted a new induction policy for members of staff who had previously been excluded – including the receptionist.

Raising the general level of awareness among all staff can make a considerable difference to the overall success of a business. Staff who know what their organization is doing and aiming to do in the future can react more positively to external customers, work with fewer misunderstandings and contribute pro-actively to its success.

One induction technique now used by some organizations is for joint sessions for people from different departments, with a different range of work responsibilities. This can create an opportunity for new staff to meet a wide variety of their colleagues and help improve inter-departmental communication in the future. This process may also help reduce barriers between management and employees.

Most companies have numbers of permanent or temporary members of staff who slip through the normal recruitment process and may therefore miss out on induction. This can include temporary receptionists, secretaries, drivers, part-timers and even job-sharers. It is important to remember the important contribution these people make to the impression of the organization in the marketplace and that they receive a suitable induction programme. A temporary receptionist, for example, will be in contact with important clients so it is certainly worth considering an appropriate induction programme. It may be possible to arrange a pool of temporary staff with a local agency who receive an induction programme before taking on any contract with your organization.

The great impact that induction and involvement can make, particularly in employees who may seem at the periphery of a business, is illustrated in the following case:

> A UK company which distributes office supplies was having difficulty recruiting and retaining good drivers. The problem did not seem to be low wages, long working hours or any other common

▶

▶

cause of complaint. Eventually, they decided to call all their existing drivers together for a meeting. 'You,' they said, 'are probably the second most important group of people in the company. We want you to know how much we value your work.' The drivers looked surprised; they had mostly not thought about their position in the company, and certainly had not thought they were important. 'Why are we important?' one asked. 'Because you meet our customers directly. The sales staff are in some ways most important, because they have regular and close contact with customers, but the drivers who deliver our products are very important too.' This thinking was a revelation to the drivers. Before long, they returned to see their manager. 'If we are important, we should wash our vans every day and have them properly cleaned every week. We also think we should have smart uniforms.' The company was only too pleased to comply with these requests; they had more satisfied employees who had begun to take a pride in their work and exhibit greater loyalty and commitment; they were also able to create a more professional impression to their customers.

Induction is a long-term process

Traditionally, induction is seen, at least, as a series of talks concentrated in one day; thereafter, training is done on the job. This approach may be inadequate. Most people find it difficult to assimilate large amounts of information in a short time and may start their job with feelings of inadequacy if they cannot remember everything they heard in a concentrated induction session.

The Japanese approach is different:

- long-term view
- induction spread over months rather than weeks
- includes periods spent working in different areas.

One of the ultimate aims of an induction programme is to create commitment and motivation. Traditional lecture-based programmes are unlikely to achieve this. Some alternatives that may be of value include:

- video on different aspects of the organization
- role playing to help team building or problem solving
- different locations
- demonstrations of work by other employees
- quizzes
- outside speakers to put your business into a global perspective or stimulate thought on the mission.

Induction is too important to be left to a small group of staff even if they are well trained. You may consider involving:

- senior managers
- skilled trainers
- immediate manager/supervisor
- variety of speakers
- a mentor or 'buddy'.

A welcoming address or session on the organization's mission by the Managing Director or other senior managers is a good foundation to show new members of the organization how much they are valued. A variety of speakers is always welcome to maintain interest in what is being said. Speakers should be selected for their attitude as well as their experience. The effort and interest displayed by them will have a direct influence on the new employee's attitude.

One of the most important relationships is that between the new employee and their immediate manager/supervisors. They should make themselves available to greet the new recruit, to show that their arrival is significant. It is a good idea to ensure that the team leader/supervisor is free to spend some time with

改

the new arrival without interruption. It may be appropriate for the new person to arrive an hour later than normal starting time on the first day so that routine matters can be dealt with first allowing few distractions.

One of the aspects of induction that the immediate manager might undertake is to make sure that everyone knows that a new member of staff is going to arrive and then introducing them to the present staff. Bear in mind that it is often difficult to remember names and it can be very disconcerting for a new employee to be continually asked who they are. It may be worth issuing name badges to the department for the first few days until everyone has learned each other's name.

A final point. One aspect of induction that has proved to be highly successful within Western organizations is that of mentoring or providing a 'buddy' to ease the new member of staff into the whole. This is so important that it deserves a chapter in its own right.

Whatever the content of an organization's new induction programme, it is important to reinforce the concept of continual improvement to the new employee by arranging regular reviews of the process during their first year.

Independent Insurance in the UK has found great success in issuing each new employee with a personal development log in which to record all their training whether on courses or, more frequently, at their desks. After four months, the new employee is asked how the training is going and the supervisor goes through the log with them.

Marks and Spencer attach great importance to their induction programme and feed back to new employees the skills that were revealed at their assessment before allocating them a store at which they will train on the job. In their fourth week, they attend a three or four day course to learn more about the retail world and Marks and Spencer in particular. After three months they have a retail induction review to help capitalize on the strengths already shown.

A leading Japanese car plant in the UK gives the following induction programme to each of its new employees:

Monday
Start formalities
History of the company
Welcome from the directors
Basic management philosophy
Lunch and welcome meeting with managers
Department visit
Manufacturing processes

Tuesday
Health and safety
Visit to production plant
Visit to administrative departments

Wednesday
Company production systems
Production system exercise
Production system video
Quality assurance
Dealer visit

Thursday
Human resources management
Teamwork development exercise
Key factors for company success
Presentation to directors

Friday
Start in department

By the end of the employees' first week, they have done a day's work, met the senior management, understood the basic management philosophy and the company history and gained a comprehensive insight into the whole operation.

改

CHECKLIST SUMMARY

Induction is a continuous process and part of the much wider process of creating an innovative and competitive organization. The process actually begins even before induction – with recruitment – and continues through on-the-job training. Induction can only be successful if the expectations raised during the first days can be met during the employment itself.

Recruitment and induction strategies need to be continually reviewed to ensure that the Kaizen approach of continual improvement is guaranteed – if the first impressions of the job are not fulfilling, it is unlikely that the new employee will be able to produce the level of work the organization is hoping for.

Points to consider:

- what does the recruitment advertising say about the organization?

- is enough time given to the selection process to ensure the best results?

- who should be involved in the selection process?

- does the induction process match the values of the organization?

- what additional elements could be included that would add value?

5

MENTORING

One aspect to induction that has existed for many years in the West and is now growing and developing into one of the most important areas of the development of the employee is mentoring.

When awareness of the Japanese techniques that were leading to their worldwide success in the 1970s and 1980s became apparent, the aspect of staff involvement and development caused some concern about how the West could adapt to the challenge. The Japanese had successfully built on their culture of mutual benefit and the sense of society membership, and Western organizations clearly had to adapt to include the individuality of their staff.

The Japanese use mentoring both formally and informally. Employees invite advice from older, more experienced staff or their managers both during working hours and, more particularly, after work. This is based in the Japanese tradition of respect for both seniority and the wisdom of elder people. It is less likely than the West to rely on one-to-one relationships, rather more on what we would classify as networking, getting to know and building relationships with many sources to whom the individual can turn for advice.

Mentoring is not confined to traditional Japanese companies. One of the most innovative ventures of recent years, known in Japan as 'Cowboy Food Discount Stores' (without

改

the connotations this would have in the West!), uses the concept of employees working in pairs – one senior and one junior – to provide effective on-the-job training.

COWBOY

COWBOY's President, Akira Nakano, believes that those on the shop floor know the market best, so he has vested them with the power to purchase and merchandise goods in order to maximize sales.

Staff spend Monday and Tuesday either in internal meetings or talking to suppliers. Wednesday is a day off followed by intensive activity on Thursday and Friday filling shelves and preparing the store for the weekend rush. Saturday and Sunday are the only days when the shops are open to customers.

There are several gains from transferring responsibility to shop floor staff:

1 High staff motivation has kept turnover at the seven COWBOY stores virtually on target.
2 Staff are motivated to sell what is on the shelves because they have selected the merchandise rather than a remote buyer.
3 Employees work in pairs – one senior and one junior – which provides ideal on-the-job training.
4 The two-day opening provides ample time for planning and preparation.

Every Monday, the Heads of Department meet with the store staff to discuss sales as well as gross profit. If sales are below target, problems are analyzed and solutions identified. Staff are given a chance to fail and learn from their mistakes – the underlying philosophy is that failure itself is an important lesson.

WINNING THE CUSTOMER

Because 60 per cent of the staff are housewives, they are in close touch with market demand, particularly from the growing ranks of dual-income households. The emphasis is not on piling the shelves high with cheap goods, but identifying product ranges that are in particular demand and then selling them at a competitive price.

Akira Nakano does not try to compete head-to-head with the long-established competition but has created a niche for low-priced, limited range weekend shopping. His staff secure low wholesale prices by returning very little stock to manufacturers – keeping in touch with customer needs ensures there is very little remaining on the shelves by Sunday evening.

The one-to-one relationship of mentoring is proving in the West to be an ideal combination of the need for involvement into the collective body of the organization while at the same time valuing and developing the individual.

Informal mentoring has taken place within organizations for many years. Whether it was the new recruit being introduced to an established member of staff to be shown around, introduced and helped to come up to performance levels as soon as possible, a formal apprenticeship scheme or the informal 'protégé' arrangements that existed in many organizations, there are countless examples of new and young members of staff being helped by more experienced colleagues.

What many organizations are discovering is that a more formal mentoring process helps activate the Kaizen attitudes in new and less experienced employees as it is based on:

- respect for the individual
- encouraging continuous improvement.

Mentoring may take several forms:

- formal, short-term induction mentoring
- formal, on-going developmental mentoring
- networking to develop different sources of advice
and support to be used when appropriate.

改

INDUCTION MENTORING

A more formal mentoring system has proved to be the touchstone for many successful organizations in the West and in many organizations this success has developed from the introduction of a more formal system of mentoring to resolve problems in the induction phase of a new employee's life.

> A major food company found that around 40 per cent of its graduates carefully chosen for their personalities and values were leaving its employment within the first six months. In some concern they called in a consultant who discovered the reason very quickly. These graduates were all extrovert, bright individuals who when sent to the more outlying regions of the food company became very lonely and isolated. Finding themselves the only graduates on site and without support, many of them handed in their resignations.

Mentoring can provide the answer to this common problem.

> **Independent Insurance**, one of Britain's faster growing insurers, has formalized the mentor approach to its induction training. As part of a more traditional approach each new employee is allocated another member of staff to look after them. This relationship allows the new member of staff to ask all the questions that they might feel unable to ask their boss and to involve the new recruit into the culture subtly and informally. Over an initial period of six months, all 284 new recruits had a mentor and the organization was delighted to discover that only three had decided not to stay.

> **Marks and Spencer** nominate a sponsor for each new employee to help them through their first few weeks and encourage them to begin to build their own networks of support.

The role of the induction mentor is therefore to:

1 Support the new employee through the confusion of the first few weeks, show them around, introduce them to other staff and help them understand how the culture works.
2 Build a relationship with the new employee to provide a basis of friendship and trust so that concerns can be speedily resolved.

An induction mentor must be willing to devote the time and attention to the role and be prepared to be as positive and open as possible to the new recruit. It is important that they completely understand and approve of the culture the organization is trying to develop.

DEVELOPMENTAL MENTORING

Induction mentoring might be described as a way of bringing a new employee up to speed effectively. What many organizations are now looking for is a way to move them forward once they are comfortable with their work.

THE KAIZEN APPROACH TO MENTORING

An organization committed to Kaizen principles will want to be developing and involving each and every one of its employees and will not be reserving a powerful tool such as mentoring for a chosen few.

The National Health Service, among many other organizations, has made mentoring a long-term support to its equal opportunities programmes. For example, many women moving into management positions have been offered a mentor to support them in their journey into previously unknown territory.

Setting up a formal wide-ranging mentoring system has its own particular needs.

THE DOUGLAS AIRCRAFT COMPANY'S MENTORING PROGRAMME

This particular case study follows a programme that is aimed at fast-trackers only (it is to be hoped that it will be extended as its success is acknowledged) but it does contain some valuable guidelines and possibilities to consider.

The Douglas Aircraft Company in California believes in the benefits of mentoring; senior management show their commitment through visible, frequent and continuing support and have built it into the business strategy. Their process follows a plan:

- the organization identifies high-performing employees
- these people are offered mentoring as a way to help define development objectives
- they are matched with executives who can help them meet their objectives
- the mentor and 'mentoree' determine goals for the relationship
- the relationship lasts one year before review and possible change.

The high-performing employees are selected on a set of criteria laid down by the parent company, as well as on readiness for promotion etc.

The potential mentors are senior managers who volunteer their time. To be considered they outline the knowledge and guidance they believe they can contribute.

The high-performing employee then selects three possible mentors from a list of those available and a steering committee (consisting of line managers, programme administrators and HR advisors) produces a final match. Their decision is based on the match between what the mentoree wants to achieve, what the mentor believes they have to offer as well as personal preference.

A single mentor will not be responsible for more than two mentorees and will not be part of the mentoree's chain of command.

Guidelines and briefing are made available to all involved in the programme to avoid any misunderstandings (for example an assumption that promotion will inevitably follow).

At the end of a year-programme, a review is held to assess progress and to plan the future. Many mentors are changed at this stage in order to find new, objective help for the following year while others have continued with the same individual for up to three years.

In a recent written survey to evaluate the programme, 80 per cent of those who responded expressed satisfaction. The biggest problem identified was that many mentors had found difficulty making enough time for the mentoree. The programme is continually being revised and improved by the steering committee following each year's survey and the participants given support and guidance to ensure its success.

Guidelines for successful formal mentoring:

- the mentor must volunteer for the role and make the necessary time available
- the mentor must have the necessary strengths and qualities to be able to contribute to the mentoree
- the mentor should not be part of the mentoree's line management
- meetings should be held at least once a month to build a relationship and give momentum to the development
- the relationship must be confidential and based on trust and respect
- the skills of both should include listening, ability to respond constructively to criticism and a commitment to set and focus on goals

- it may or may not include personal issues; the organization should give guidelines
- if the relationship is becoming too personal or breaking down, there should be a procedure to deal with it.

The role of the mentor includes:

- communicator to encourage two-way communication, listen to ideas or career concerns and respond appropriately, plus schedule clear time to meet
- coach to work with mentoree to identify skills, values and interests, evaluate options and set strategies, to develop skills and qualities to achieve goals
- advisor to give input on options, opportunities available and clarify any misunderstandings
- networker to develop the mentoree's contacts and relationships to create opportunities
- advocate to intervene on the mentoree's behalf to resolve difficulties or create opportunities.

The actual mentoring process itself, as already stated, should take place at least once a month.

The first meeting might involve the mentoree and their immediate supervisor having a personal development session to set goals that will tie the mentoring programme into the needs of the department. It is valuable to link the supervisor to the scheme so that they feel involved and able to support its success. In some schemes the mentor might contact the supervisor directly to discuss suitable directions for the programme but this can have drawbacks in that the mentoree may not want communication to take place behind his or her back. One of the keys to mentoring success is that it is objective and the mentoree has the freedom to be completely open and honest.

The first formal mentoring session will then focus on the objectives brought by the mentoree. The discussions can act as an ice-breaker and clarify each side's expectations of the relationship. Together they need to develop simple goals for the programme and their relationship. At this stage, the mentor may be able to suggest additional training or development opportunities to achieve the goal.

Regular meetings will take place to review progress on the achievement of the goal, give additional coaching, revise goals and set new ones as well as reviewing regularly the personal process between them. The relationship needs to be two-way and adapted where possible to achieve the best results.

Failure in the relationship should not be viewed as a problem but rather a learning experience for both parties, and new partners should be found for each as soon as possible to support the programme and rebuild confidence. Some training may well be helpful before introducing such a system into an organization changing its culture from authoritarian to developmental.

The benefits of mentoring include:

- development on a one-to-one basis at a speed and level appropriate to the individual
- sending a genuine message of care, support and value to the individual as well as confidence of future advancement and success
- building good relationships between departments and levels of seniority
- allowing the mentoree to express goals and ambitions that they might find dangerous in their department
- helping staff to acknowledge mistakes quickly and learn from them
- encouraging the Kaizen goal of continuous improvement proven success in the West, embracing and developing the culture of individuality.

己欠

CHECKLIST SUMMARY

1 Mentoring is a valuable tool in creating the balance necessary in the West between the collective and the individual.

2 Mentoring shares similar values to Kaizen and can be considered as a useful tool in implementing Kaizen in an organization.

3 Consider introducing more formal mentoring programmes, both induction and developmental.

4 Encourage mentoring but avoid making it compulsory.

5 Gain commitment from senior management and encourage them to take part.

6

TEAMWORKING

One of the key elements of the 'quality people' approach is to provide them with the conditions where they can flourish. In the East, teamworking has long been the most effective way of doing this, and increasingly in the West, the benefits of teamworking are also being recognized.

A large proportion of Western organizations have now introduced teamworking in one form or another and have been amazed at the positive differences it has made; others have been disappointed by their results. To succeed, it is essential that organizations consider all the factors that make teamworking successful.

TEXAS INSTRUMENTS

One of very many organizations who have been disappointed was Texas Instruments Defense Systems and Electronics Group who in 1991 decided to learn from their experience and rethink the entire process. Earlier, management had responded to the promises of total-quality management by pushing for the creation of teams. These had been created with little understanding of the other changes that would be needed to support their introduction. Without supervision, adequate training, clear objectives or understanding of customer needs, many of the earlier teams had been ineffectual. Theirs is not an isolated example by any account.

But once Texas Instruments had rethought the process, aligned

▶

▶
> the entire organization to their strategy and put right the past mistakes, within six months they achieved:
>
> ● 50 per cent reduction in cycle time
> ● 60 per cent reduction in scrap
> ● 30 per cent improvement in productivity.

So what are some of the fundamental lessons to be considered before introducing successful teamworking?

WHAT IS A TEAM?

'Light is the task when many share the toil'

Homer

The classic definition (from Bernard Babington Smith, *Training in Small Groups*) is:

> 'A group in which the individuals have a common aim and in which the jobs and skills of each member fit in with those of others as – to take a very mechanical and static analogy – in a jigsaw puzzle, pieces fit together without distortion and together produce an overall pattern.'

We might say then that team members can complement each other and that a team can produce more than the sum of individual components. Teamworking can provide for an organization a way of achieving more from the same resources. Teams are a vital structure therefore for organizations which want to adopt Kaizen principles.

John Adair in his book *Effective Teambuilding* adds that the two strands in this definition – a common task and complementary contributions – are essential to the concept of a team. An effective team may be defined as one that achieves its aim in the most efficient way and is then ready to take on more challenging tasks if so required.

COMMITMENT OF SENIOR MANAGEMENT

The first and most important element required for the successful introduction of teamworking is that senior management must be committed and enthusiastic. One of the key factors for success is how teamworking is perceived by management. If the management consider teamworking is:

- a very successful way of getting the best from individuals
- a way to tap creativity and increase commitment by encouraging close relationships and added responsibility
- a way to higher productivity, better quality and greater efficiency

then it is obviously a great deal more likely to be successful than if they consider that teams add nothing to organizations except more cynicism and confusion.

WHY TEAMWORKING?

It is unfortunately a common occurrence for organizations to introduce teams without anyone knowing or understanding why. So the question 'Why teams?' needs careful consideration.

Senior management needs to be committed to the idea of achieving better business performance through the effective use of teams or there will be little benefit from teamworking.

改

When teams are well set up and clearly focused, they have been proved to lead to:

- higher productivity
- more new ideas
- greater employee satisfaction and motivation
- higher and more consistent performance.

However, without that clear focus, there is no guarantee that teams will produce these achievements.

DAIICHI HOTEL

Tokyo's Daiichi Hotel Annex was voted number one in a recent customer satisfaction survey and believes that the way it successfully introduced teamworking is largely responsible.

The hotel staff are divided into three teams:

- room related
- eating and drinking
- cooking.

Within each team, staff cover all specific job functions. For example, within the room-related team, the concierge, bell-boy and receptionist all cover for each other at busy times, or when something unusual happens. The company training manual compares this approach to that of a successful baseball team where players with specialist skills also provide support for other team members. The Daiichi Hotel believes that:

- teamworking can make an important contribution to customer satisfaction
- multiskilling can be used to improve service levels
- good team members support each other in busy periods.

DETTMERS INDUSTRIES

US manufacturer, Dettmers Industries, makes seating and tables for the aviation industry. The company is an advanced exponent of teamworking and has very successfully developed the concept in a way it has found appropriate to its own needs. In 1993 it was voted one of the best small firms to work for by *Inc.* magazine.

Dettmers believe that employees can be very creative if they are given the opportunity ... and the education. Too often, they believe, organizations start from the premise that people are stupid and incapable of contributing or planning ideas. But by introducing teamworking and then focusing the company's education system on these teams, Dettmers have brought the social element back into learning.

Teams at Dettmers go further than in most organizations: they are responsible for hiring their own personnel, electing their own leaders, setting their own schedules and even deciding their own salaries. Organizing the workforce into multidisciplinary teams responsible for the total manufacturing process has led to improvements in productivity (deliveries, for example, now take 25 days instead of the industry average of 60 days), quality and innovation.

Dettmers gives the team the right to decide when they want to recruit a new member who is then taken on for a three-month introductory period during which they are paid less than the market rate. During this period, they learn the team skills and get to understand the Dettmers' philosophy. The team votes after three months whether to include the new member permanently. From this point on, they will earn their salary in the same way as established team members and usually make up the deficit within a few months. The company believes that applicants who are prepared to start at a lower rate are looking for 'more than just a job'.

Dettmers believe their experience proves that teamworking:

- provides tangible business benefits

- proves that with education and the right conditions employees can and will make a contribution
- provides discipline and values to help improve the standards and performance of all employees
- team-based pay with a tangible reward for effort can maintain team performance.

ARE WE ALREADY TEAMWORKING?

Organizations are sometimes unsure whether they have teams or simply groups of people working together. It is certainly true to say that any group of people who do not know they are a team cannot be one. To become a team, a group of individuals needs to have a strong common purpose and to work towards that purpose together rather than individually. They need also to believe that they will achieve more by co-operating than working individually.

It is essential to achieve a positive balance between the effectiveness of the team and the individuality of its members.

Team needs
- Shared or compatible values.
- Shared or compatible purpose.
- Responsibility for each other's development.
- Mutual respect and trust.
- A shared skill base.
- Collective ownership.

Individual members' needs
- Understanding of differences in performance requirements.

- Understanding and esteem for individual differences.

Successful teams should be broad enough in spirit to cope with conflicts arising from these differing demands.

Although teams share the general attitudes listed above, in other respects they can be considerably different. Here is just one example, a comparison between a production team and a product development team.

Production team	*Product development team*
• Short-term schedules with varying degrees of pressure.	• Longer-term perspective, with pressures less definable.
• Internal focus.	• External focus.
• Work relatively monotonous.	• Creative possibilities, especially in early stages of project.
• Skills primarily functional.	• Broader skills.
• Limited working flexibility.	• Considerable flexibility of approach.
• Interdependence immediate and high.	• Interdependence high but less immediate.
• Members work in close proximity, often from the same social environment.	• Longer periods of working separately, with varied backgrounds.
• Issues such as safety crucial.	• Different issues will be important.
• Autonomy limited.	• Considerable degree of autonomy.
• Measures and methods of performance clear, precise and immediate.	• Methods and measures of performance less tangible in short term. More complex level of risk in collective purpose.
• Competition between team members low.	• Competition between team members greater, though less visible.

A sporting analogy may make these crucial differences between teams clearer, comparing the difference between a rugby team and a tennis team.

The rugby pack has an intense, brief, continuous level of interdependence so that they operate as a single unit. They have to train and play together in a uniquely co-operative way. Emphasis on individual skill will not be high, yet there can be a

改

considerable range of skills at work within the pack. The ability to work together is fundamental to the effective performance of the group.

A tennis team, on the other hand, is based on a collection of individuals working separately for the collective achievement of the team. Training will be more individually based. Emphasis on individual skills is likely to be higher and the limits of people's skills will be more defined. Individualism can flourish and interdependence will be looser.

Because there are such significant differences between different types of team, a 'blanket' approach to team management is dangerous. Identifying the appropriate style of management and participation at an early stage will help to maximize results and reduce the risk of later disappointment or failure.

INVOLVING THE WHOLE ORGANIZATION IN TEAMS

The understanding, support and participation of the entire organization, particularly senior managers, is essential in setting up a team programme.

Ideally, all staff should have the opportunity of teamworking, and managers should have teamworking projects underway to demonstrate their own understanding of the process and to share the experience. One of the most useful things a management group can do is to lead by example – form a successful team and show the rest of the organization what can be achieved.

Provide the right environment

To demonstrate management's commitment to a people-based culture, it helps to make small but visible changes.

ASHTON PHOTO INC.

One example of success is Ashton Photo Inc. of Oregon USA whose strategy includes changing the working environment deliberately to improve relationships. It is now a workplace without walls – literally. Staff can walk anywhere, including into the finance department and the factory floor. The President of the company has installed an aquarium next to his office to encourage people to visit him. All meetings are open and everyone is welcome to attend. Basketball courts and paths through the gardens for employees to use for leisure during breaks are being built. A relaxation room with a couch, pillows and music is available for anyone feeling unwell or wishing to catch up on their sleep during a break. And the very best office in the building is now redecorated and called the 'Vanilla Room' which is available on a first come first served basis for any member of staff who wishes to use it for the day.

Has it worked? The CEO certainly thinks so as productivity has risen 60 per cent since 1985, sales have doubled and a genuine spirit of teamwork and employee involvement exists.

Many organizations might flinch from doing quite the same thing, but to change the working environment, even only a little, is a very cost-effective way to show things are changing dramatically.

Team groupings within organizations

If you take any group of people, you will find there are many ways in which they can be formed into smaller units or groups. Within organizations, there are three common ways in which groups can be formed:

1 From within the same work area.
2 From different departments or divisions.
3 From different levels of the organization.

改

Each will have different purposes, different problems and different make-ups, and it is essential that these issues are explicitly dealt with when the team is set up.

GIVING THE TEAM A CLEAR PURPOSE

The success of a team depends on a purpose that is clear, relevant and accepted by the members.

Without a clearly understood purpose, people have no goal to strive for, so the management team needs to formulate a clear vision. The team vision must reflect the overall corporate vision but ideally will allow the team to operate like a small entrepreneurial company in its own right.

Ideally the goal should be generated from within the group. If it is imposed by someone outside who has no real understanding of the group's strengths and weaknesses, it could be counter-productive. However, with the right level of motivation, education and support from outside, the group can sometimes reach levels of achievement beyond their initial conceptions.

HOW A SONY TEAM SET ITS GOAL

The Sony project team responsible for the Data Discman had a unique set of nine guiding principles:

1 Believe everything can be half the size you initially thought of.
2 Decide what size the product should be, even before considering what it should consist of.
3 Set a clear, simple target.
4 Agree the target and motivate yourself for success before considering the detailed substance of the project or product.

5 'Difficult' means possible, the term 'impossible' should be excluded from the discussion.
6 Before explaining or attempting to explain the idea, make the product.
7 Brainstorm in your hotel, do not end your discussion or return to work before your discussions are ended.
8 The most promising of ideas must be kept secret from your boss; you must make the product before telling him or her.
9 If you want help, ask the busiest people; they are the ones who will have the best ideas.

Source: Simon Collinson, Institute for Japanese-European Technology studies, University of Edinburgh, in *Technology Analysis and Strategic Management*, Vol 5, No 3, 1993.

Some of these principles are radical, but they show that motivation and team spirit can achieve extraordinary results. Remember these are goals set by the teams themselves, they are not imposed from outside and, in many cases, the team is so confident of success that it will play down its progress until it is ready to reveal its achievement.

INTRODUCING TEAMS

Before looking in detail at introducing a team, it is important to make sure that the following overall organizational issues have been satisfactorily resolved:

- the overall strategy
- organization vision and values
- an integrated and coherent people policy, including the key issues of pay structure and development opportunities.

Experience indicates that teamwork generally fails because these fundamental issues have not been addressed. Part of the explanation lies in the fact that organizations need to be constantly changing in response to pressures from the external environment, yet people within them feel the need for stability and may, in reality, resist these changes.

Resolving the big 'corporate' issues and communicating them openly to the whole organization is fundamental to the effectiveness of the smaller team unit.

Setting levels of autonomy

The right level of autonomy is crucial to the success of teamwork. Ideally it should be a balance with which both management and staff feel comfortable.

There is no ideal level of autonomy. Much depends on the organization's experience in teamworking and the type of work the team will undertake. Achieving a high level of autonomy requires careful handling of expectations, together with extensive training and experiment over a period of time. The table below shows two extremes – each of them may be appropriate to different stages of teamwork development.

Total autonomy
(Operates as a minibusiness -
  suitable for mature teams)

- selects own members
- operates its own division
- responsible for its own
  budgets and expenditure.

Limited autonomy
(Autonomy limited by
  management – suitable for
  fledgling teams)
- specific remit
- specific operation methods.

Dettmers Industries, described earlier in this chapter, is an advanced exponent of teamworking and has delegated the following autonomy to its teams:

- elect their own leaders
- hire their own personnel
- set their own schedules
- responsible for product as well as process improvements
- compensation is team-based.

Other companies use teams in a more formalized way.

PROSPECT FOODS LTD

Prospect Foods Ltd is a family business which is best known for its five café tearooms in North Yorkshire, 'Betty's' and 'Taylors Tearooms', although it also operates a high-class bakery and a tea and coffee packing business.

Faced in the late 1980s with staff turnover problems and lower profitability, the company developed a Group Operational Plan as the cornerstone of its business. The core plan which each business area has gives rise to performance objectives, which are cascaded down through the company, so every employee has a clear vision of their targets and the standards for achieving them. The process is supported by a comprehensive training programme.

Particularly noteworthy in the context of teamworking is the system of team briefings. A comprehensive and rapid team-building process occurs every month. At 7.30am on the third Tuesday of every month senior managers are briefed. By Thursday afternoon the same week, all 670 staff (organized in teams of up to 10 people) have had their own team briefing.

Each team briefing lasts around 40 minutes and covers '4 Ps':
- Progress, including financial results
- People - personal changes which have taken place
- Policy issues
- Points for action.

Source: Adapted from '*The Benefits of Being an Investor in People*', Investors in People

Setting levels of perfofmance

Teams are capable of giving far more than most organizations understand or are ready to allow. Probably the most valid and effective performance levels are those defined by the teams themselves.

Measuring the performance of individuals and teams is important but it needs to be treated with caution. In a period of intense competition when the 'bottom line' and short-term results are seen as significant, it is vital that performance criteria are not oversimplified.

Performance criteria – key considerations:

- visible results need to be balanced with process aspects such as communication and the capacity to motivate
- there should be both short- and medium-term criteria
- both individual and team performance criteria are important
- context needs to be taken into account in selecting criteria.

Probably the most valid and effective performance criteria are those established by the team members themselves. Experience indicates that teams are more likely to be over-demanding of themselves than to set limits that are too low. In fact, teams are capable of giving far more than most organizations understand or are ready to allow. People's perception of what is possible is often limited by their own perception or experience.

A vital point of Kaizen is to analyze and measure, so that new higher standards can be set. This process needs to be applied to the work that teams are doing, measuring for example:

- the time taken from planning to production
- the number of queries satisfactorily handled in a day

- the number of complaints about a product received in a month
- the proportion of satisfied customers returning to a hotel for a further stay, etc etc.

The PDCA cycle

In order to practice improvement in a systematic way it is necessary to follow a cycle of activities on a regular basis. This has become known as the PDCA cycle, Plan, Do, Check, Action. These four steps correspond closely to Deming's production wheel, which stressed the interaction between Research, Design, Production and Sales, which should be in constant rotation for the purpose of improving customer satisfaction through better quality. The steps of the cycle also corresponded to specific management actions.

Relationship between Deming's wheel and the PDCA cycle

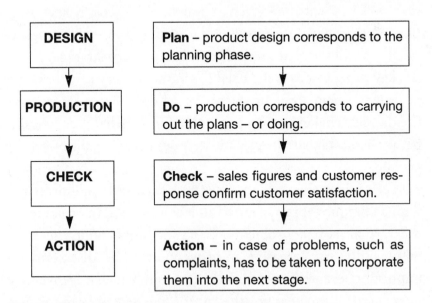

Source: Imai 'Kaizen: the Key to Japan's Competitive Success' (1986)

In this case Deming's research stage is also part of the planning stage before or in the process of design.

The Whole Process

The process begins with a clear description of the current situation, the collection of relevant data. This forms the basis of the design for production. During production and after sales checks are made and the results analyzed in order to upgrade the system. The process is a continuum. It can be applied at every level and department of an organization, in different degrees. At the upper echelon, the focus will be strategic. At the middle level this will be for the medium-term business issues; at the next level, short- to medium-term issues and for front-line management and staff, daily management of 'local' issues. Each stage requires clear objectives and measures, all of which should interconnect, so that front-line staff will make their contribution within the overall strategic framework. If, for example, there is a cost-cutting exercise companywide, cost reduction at the micro level will form part of the remit of Kaizen or improvement activities at that level. The deployment of strategic policy is a key issue, just as is the need for input at every level upwards in order to help strategic decisions. Middle management have the difficult challenge of acting as a filter for what is practicable between the highest level and the operational realities on the ground.

Each stage in the cycle requires particular skills and practices, with techniques appropriate to all levels of staff. In broad terms they are all either 'problem solving' or 'opportunity development skills' for 'creative improvement'. The distinction is important because it describes the extent to which improvement is 'reductive', or 'creative', the latter often necessary in the process of profound change.

The PDCS cycle

The next cycle in the improvement process is the PDCS cycle, S meaning 'Standardize'. The purpose of this cycle is to provide new standards for the entire production-process/product-service. Standardization is crucial. It should be noted however, that in conjunction with standardization, there is a requirement to understand the nature of variation. This fundamental point, which Deming regarded as more important than any other, requires profound knowledge about variation, in particular the ability to separate variations due to 'special causes', which require special action, and those which are due to common causes and will therefore require a change in the system's design and operation. Deming's famous experiment with the red beads (for details, contact the British Deming Association) provides an excellent case of how misplaced thinking about variation often is, leading to counterproductive results.

Measuring Performance

Teams will also want to measure their own performance, and will need to find the method most suitable to their own team at any particular time. Various tools are commonly used to measure, and hence offer opportunities to improve performance:

- questionnaires
- individual interviews or group interviews
- observation
- existing data.

Although on a regular basis the most useful element to measure tends to be the achievement of results, in certain circumstances teams may wish to measure aspects such as:

- to what extent do all team members understand the objectives of the team
- is the current team structure the most effective possible

- how effective is the team leadership (does the leader motivate well, listen to sugestions, delegate as far as possible, inform and educate, etc)
- how many problems has the team dealt with and how effectively
- does the team deal well with conflict
- how effective is the team in communication
- is the team sufficiently well-trained, creative, full of suggestions, etc.

To ensure co-operation in any measuring activity, it is important to involve all team members in setting the measurement levels, deciding what is worth measuring, and in sharing the results. This is an area where the trust, so necessary in Kaizen organizations, can easily break down, and all efforts should be made to prevent this, by openness and straightforward behaviour.

In order to measure themselves effectively, not only managers but also team members need to be trained to use standard statistical tools, such as cause and effect analysis, Pareto analysis and process flow checking.

The true extent to which individuals and therefore teams can contribute positively is greatly undervalued. The smart organizations understand this and have created a dynamic environment of considerable team autonomy, based on extensive and profound personal transformation education.

Guidelines for team selection and operation

Variety of skill, experience and personality will contribute to a balanced team, though all team members need to recognize the importance of valuing differences

The selection factors are clearly driven by the purpose of the team, but some guidelines may help enhance team selection:

- where teams are composed of people from the same area, special importance needs to be placed on the cohesion and compatibility of the group
- when new members are selected, existing team members should be closely involved
- this level of involvement may require training for team members and may require a trial period
- team-building activities outside the work area and any activities that bring about group involvement should be encouraged
- in cross-functional teams and project teams, or where the team remit is short term, less emphasis needs to be placed on group stability through compatibility of personality
- an environment of dynamic challenge may well contribute to higher performance and stimulate development.

One aspect which can frequently cause difficulties is that most individuals will choose to work and build relationships with people similar to them. In team selection this can lead to a group of identical individuals who are missing the differences that develop creativity. The watchword is 'complementary' rather than 'identical'. To return to the sports team analogy, no team will be effective if it has all attacking players, it needs a balance of players superb in their particular role; ie a mixture of attacking, play-building and defending.

R. Meredith Belbin in his book *Management Teams – Why they succeed or fail*, has identified eight core types which are valuable to have in a team:

Type	Typical features
Company worker	conservative, dutiful, predictable

Qualities: organizing abilities, practical common sense, hard-working, self-discipline.

Chairman   calm, self-confident, controlled

Qualities: a capacity for treating and welcoming all potential contributors on their merits, without prejudice. A strong sense of objectives.

Shaper   highly strung, outgoing, dynamic

Qualities: drive and a readiness to challenge inertia, ineffectiveness, complacency or self-deception.

Plant   individualistic, serious-minded, unorthodox

Qualities: genius, imagination, intellect, knowledge.

Resource Investigator   extroverted, enthusiastic, curious, communicative

Qualities: a capacity for contacting people and exploring anything new. An ability to respond to challenge.

Monitor/Evaluator   sober, unemotional, prudent

Qualities: judgement, discretion, hard-headedness.

Team Worker   socially-orientated, rather mild, sensitive

Qualities: an ability to respond to people and to situations, and to promote team spirit.

Completer/Finisher   painstaking, orderly, conscientious, anxious

Qualities: a capacity for follow-through. Perfectionism.

Every individual will have aspects of each of these types in their character and in different teams or conditions may display them differently. What is important is to recognize the value of each of these roles and build teams, where possible, to encourage each aspect to be represented.

How many people should be in a team?

The answers from different organizations as to what is the perfect number vary from between four and fifteen depending on a whole range of variables. Fifteen is about the maximum number of people anyone can communicate with without having to raise their voice significantly and any less than four has a restriction in the amount of creativity and variety that can be produced. It is interesting to note that these figures range between the maximum and minimum numbers of sports teams – perhaps less of a coincidence than it seems.

Guidelines on team meetings

Meetings are an integral part of teamworking and though there are no firm rules on frequency, these guidelines may prove helpful:

- achieve a balance between having meetings sufficiently close together to maintain momentum and interest, and leaving a sufficient gap for fact finding and normal work activities.
- one meeting of 30 or even 60 minutes a week is a common approach for teams working together on improvement programmes. This might increase to twice a week near the completion of a project.
- in some manufacturing organizations, there are daily meetings though their purpose is usually short-term schedule and task-orientated, rather than longer-term problem solving or process related.
- there should be sufficient time to give people reasonable warning of a meeting but the meeting should never be too far ahead.

Guidelines on meeting venue and times

The venue for a meeting can have a significant effect on the performance and outcome of a meeting, so it is important that an

改

appropriate environment should be available. The timing of meetings is equally important, since the time of the day and the day of the week affect people in different ways. Friday afternoons and Monday mornings are traditionally favoured slots for meetings, but timing should depend on individual circumstances.

> **Nissan UK** have purpose-built a series of large meeting areas, one for each team. All the areas are spacious, well-lit, have notice boards and tea and coffee-making facilities. According to Nissan 'it is difficult to underestimate the importance of these areas'.

The 'wilt factor' can also have an impact on the effectiveness of meetings. People often tire of regular meetings and the whole process loses impetus.

> **BP** tackled this problem by finding new, unique, phrases to describe different sorts of meetings and to avoid using the 'm' word that was tending to induce a glazed look in some of its staff. A 'huddle' is a weekly meeting of the key staff in a department while a 'cuddle' is the monthly meeting of all department staff.

> **The Jardinerie Garden Centre** in Cheshire set up project improvement groups (or PIGs for short) and one of these 'piglets' was given the task of setting up a security system to cut down on pilferage. This 'piglet' recommended a new system of security tagging which included checking employees' bags. Staff were happy to agree to this because their representatives had been responsible for suggesting it, something the management would have been loath to even discuss for fear of an angry response.

UNDERSTANDING LIFE CYCLES

Cycles have an impact on all aspects of life and they are a significant fact in determining the successful outcome of teamworking. There are two ways of looking at the team life-cycle – the life of the team itself and the life of the project:

Team life cycle
- Formation
- Establishment
- Operating
- Maximum performance
- Fall off in performance
- Disbandment

Project life cycle
- Initial idea
- Early development
- Definition of purpose
- Implementation
- Evaluation

It is worth drawing attention to the fact that in the team life-cycle, very soon after the team has achieved maximum performance, it begins to lose momentum and drop in output. It is this moment of high performance that the team leader needs to recognize and take action to begin a new life-cycle before output drops too rapidly. This may be done by introducing a new member or re-evaluating the goals and targets.

It is important to recognize that, psychologically, people's response will be different at each stage of the process and it will also vary according to their specific role or capacity to contribute.

Team records

Keeping records of team activities is a useful way of monitoring the learning and evolutionary progress of the team. It also encourages openness and allows each member to learn from the experience. When a team is actively working on a project, details of its approach and methods can be a valuable future record.

These records can be kept by one or more team member and rotated as any other tasks are. They should not however be used for assessment, except by the team itself to clarify issues or overcome difficulties for its own benefit. The aim is to build confidence and learn through shared experience.

Team roles

Specific roles will vary according to the type of team, its goals, the stages of development and its composition. The simplest roles to define are:

- leaders
- facilitators
- recorders.

There is an important distinction between roles within and outside the team.

Internal roles: the part people play in the actual operation of the team

External roles: the roles that are allocated outside the main group.

For both roles, it is important that everyone knows what is expected of them, and that what is expected is reasonable and attainable. They should also know that what they are given to do is appropriate to their duties.

Outside expertise can be useful, not to lead the team, but to provide extra information or to work on specific areas within the team. The Shell UK team that devises global scenarios has considerable experience in drawing on outside expertise. They consult:

- world business leaders
- journalists

- politicians
- educators
- representatives and teams from within other Shell companies.

This process is part of a massive global data gathering and analysis operation that is used to draw up global scenarios which are then used by all product and regional divisions to help in future business planning.

Time

A final cautionary note. Transforming any organization takes time, it takes patience, it takes constant adaptions and continual improvement. The West has long jumped at potential 'answers' and thrown the baby out with the bathwater. Teams have been around for many hundreds of years, they just have not always been very effective. It takes time and patience to succeed – but as the examples quoted show – the rewards can outweigh any costs if you can succeed eventually.

CHECKLIST SUMMARY

1 As in all aspects of a people-centred approach, the commitment of senior management is vital.

2 It is important to consider why teamwork is being introduced and to ensure that they are all genuine teams balanced between the individual and the collective needs.

3 Involve the whole organization in teamworking and consider the benefits and drawbacks of differing groupings of people.

4 Make sure teamworking has a clear purpose in your organization.

5 Set appropriate levels of autonomy for the organization and the maturity of the teams.

6 Set appropriate levels and measurement of performance.

7 Give support and training to all groups to ensure that the processes support the achievement of the organization's goals.

8 Be patient and allow time.

7

TEAM
LEADERSHIP

Probably the most consistently important attributes of leadership are to have the trust of team members and the ability to motivate

In an environment where creativity and flexibility are to flourish, there is no single 'right' style of team leadership. For example, strong, highly-directional leadership may be necessary in difficult conditions, while high-participatory leadership may be appropriate to others. Leaders have to be flexible and responsive to deal with changing situations. Human skills are as important and sometimes more important than functional skills.

John Adair, the British writer on leadership topics, in his work on teams identifies the role of Team Leader as being responsible for three main areas that interlap so that they balance to achieve the maximum effectiveness. Too often the task has been focused on, to the detriment of team and individual which in turn causes the task to suffer.

Achieving the task will include: analyzing the skills and training required as well as encouraging a Kaizen approach to continually improving the efficiency and quality with which the task is achieved.

Building and maintaining the team will include: arranging regular meetings to ensure communication, building social as well as task opportunities to encourage bonding and the building of good relationships and ensuring that time and attention is given to the process, how the task is actually achieved, and encouraging its continual improvement and development.

Developing the individual will include motivation, personal development, training and support. Similarly to task and team, it requires a continual on-going improvement process. Some of the results of the work of two of the best known researchers into motivation fit well with the Kaizen model.

Frederick Herzberg, an American researcher into working processes, found that the elements that contributed to high morale and job satisfaction were:

- a sense of achievement
- recognition
- responsibility
- promotion prospects
- the nature of the work itself

and that the elements (he called them 'hygiene factors' as they go unrecognized when they are good but) whose absence or inadequacy in a job produces dissatisfaction and poor performance were:

- head office policy
- pay
- type of management
- working conditions
- relationships with others
- fringe benefits.

Abraham Maslow, the American psychologist, worked on the hierarchy of human needs suggests that an individual has to fulfil each level of need before attaining self-fulfilment:

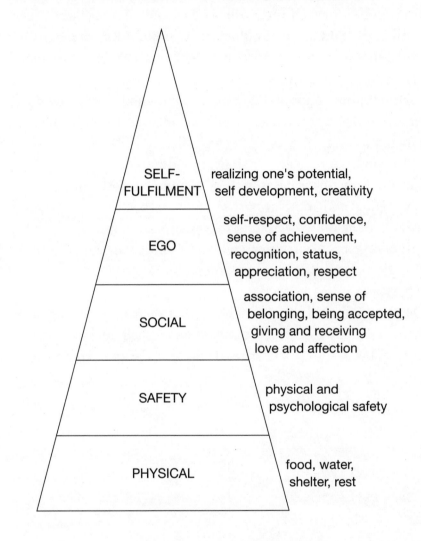

Many of the motivating factors identified can be fulfilled within a teamworking environment and it is part of the role of the team leader to be aware of them and work with each individual to encourage their continual improvement.

改

QUALITIES REQUIRED OF A TEAM LEADER

Self-awareness is a key factor and one that is often overlooked. Team leaders of the future will need to look more closely at personal issues and use psychological skills and tools as a basis for expanding their perceptions in order to improve their own and their team's performance.

Developing, supporting and encouraging team members requires a high degree of sophistication in personal skills including communication, empathy, listening skills and a lack of prejudice.

A team leader's role is significantly different from that of the old-style supervisor because there is a much greater emphasis on developing and motivating the team, rather than performing specific work duties. Existing supervisors are not necessarily the best people to become team leaders. Companies which want to change their culture need to do much more than rename their supervisors as team leaders.

Japanese team leaders often say that their proudest achievement is if they can develop members of their team to surpass them. This is a long way from the old role of the supervisor.

OPEL

Opel, the German car manufacturer, defines the role of its team leaders as

- to motivate the team
- reconcile any differences within the team
- represent the views of the team with third parties
- summon technical assistance when necessary
- ensure that team targets are met.

HOTPOINT

Hotpoint is the UK's most successful white goods manufacturer and a key player in the markets for refrigerators, washing machines, tumble dryers and dishwashers. It employs around 6,000 people in three factories, 21 service offices and 8 depots.

Although the company was increasing its market share in the 1980s, competition was becoming more severe and it realized that it would need to change its work methods and management style in order to survive and prosper.

Its first attempt – a TQM programme launched in 1989 – failed because of an approach which focused on top-down statements. The company therefore devised a new strategy in which all employees were to participate and which would concentrate on responding to customers. Key elements of the programme included:

- reduction in the number of reporting levels
- leadership and monitoring to replace top-down control; people are given clear objectives and the necessary support
- introduction of team working throughout the company
- team objectives largely defined by the team leader with guidance from directors
- wide-ranging and regular training for team-leaders (200 now appointed) to help them take greater responsibility for quality and performance
- company plans renewed annually, and leading to departmental and individual plans
- increase in internal training, new appraisal system, training audits, etc.

The new approach has borne fruit for Hotpoint:

- annual cost savings of nearly £2 million in the Peterborough factory
- response time from customer order to delivery reduced from 19 to 4 weeks

- 'Frost-Free' fridge design improvements speeded up to 9 months (instead of 15 months) thanks to the involvement of multi-function project teams
- increase in profit, despite a fall in sales.

As a result of these changes, Hotpoint at Peterborough is now performing as well as the General Electrics plant at Louisville in the USA (Hotpoint is a joint venture between GEC and General Electric of the USA), and their aim is to continue the improvements.

Based on '*The Benefits of Being an Investor in People*', Investors in People

RECONCILING DIFFERENCES WITHIN THE TEAM

It is very likely that a team of individuals displaying the sort of characteristics identified by Belbin will regularly have disagreements. The role of the team leader will normally be to facilitate and draw the team's attention to the valuing of other opinions in order to produce an outcome that is best for each individual, the team and the organization. Creative tension should not be feared but, rather, welcomed and used constructively to make major improvements or encourage innovation. It is just this sort of creativity in partnership with the hundreds of thousands of small improvements (Kaizen) that unites the best of the West with the best of the East.

Occasionally a team will suffer a complete breakdown. This may happen for many reasons and often the introduction of a new team member or project will resolve it.

But what can a team leader do if the problem is with one individual who seems unwilling to play his or her full part in the team? It must be stressed that most individuals are by nature responsive to a teamworking environment and work out for themselves how best to benefit from it. Rarely an individual, who might be described as a 'loner', can see no benefit in it and refuses to contribute. When the team leader has fully assessed the situation, considered whether it is a lack of understanding by him or herself or others and whether there is a human or work need that is not being fulfilled, he or she should ask the individual concerned what they would suggest. Often the individual is the only one who can suggest a solution and very occasionally it may be that they decide jointly that teamworking is not appropriate and try to find them a position within the organization where they can perform to their potential. Individual 'loners' may have a considerable amount to offer their organization and it is to be recommended that organizations should be flexible enough to try to accommodate their needs if the potential contribution justifies it.

TEAM LEADERSHIP IN NISSAN

Effective team leaders are critical to the success of teamworking at Nissan UK. To ensure the right calibre, the company selects them carefully, provides them with comprehensive training and pays them well.

Nissan calls its more than 200 team leaders 'supervisors' which is very confusing as their roles, which include the following, have very little in common with a traditional supervisor.

- recruitment
- training
- communication
- maintaining morale
- quality
- balanced workload
- supervising suppliers and subcontractors.

▶

As well as achieving production targets, they also have to manage the team and look for improvements in all processes that are the team's responsibility. They do not stay with the team they have created for long; to keep them fresh and to broaden their experience, they move to different teams at intervals.

Because a Nissan supervisor is responsible for all aspects of people management, there is a pronounced emphasis on people skills to enable them to select the right staff, make the verbal job offers, provide the right training to meet quality and production standards as well as appraising and motivating all team members.

Balancing motivation and control is seen as crucial to team performance.

Motivation only	**Control only**
Leads to people doing what they think is right but can lead to anarchy.	Control from the top down without motivation can lead to alienation.

Nissan supervisors have overall responsibility for quality and continuous improvement. Each employee is encouraged and trained not to pass mistakes onto the next 'internal customer' without highlighting them and the supervisor measures quality performance. If a car gets through to a department without any form of repair, they have achieved the quality objective.

To encourage continuous improvement, Nissan's supervisors are responsible for determining how jobs are done within their section. They are told how a car will enter their section and how it should leave. How they tackle or improve the job is at their discretion, although certain safety-critical tasks are excluded.

Team told what condition the car will enter their section in	**Opportunity for continuous improvement**	Team told what condition the car must leave their section in

Nissan UK operates a modular training and development pro-gramme which covers core skills as well as skills specific to the post of 'supervisor'. The initial development programme covers:

- company induction
- department induction
- company wide support
- running the job
- people management
- technical training
- job specific technical modules.

LEADERLESS TEAMS?

Organizations which have operated teamworking for some years are increasingly questioning the role of team leaders and asking whether they are even necessary. Team leaders who have developed their teams effectively should have the confidence to delegate leadership to any member of the team.

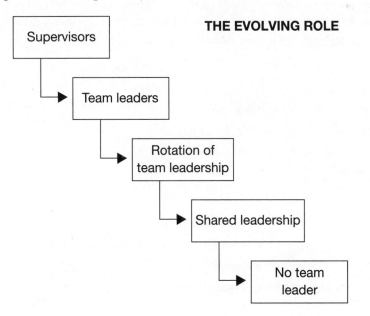

Towards self-managed teams

In the self-managed team, there is a different form of relationship. The team may need a leader or coach to support it, but essentially it makes its own day-to-day decisions, normally in relation to overall corporate targets. The approach has been successfully used in financial services and telecommunications as well as manufacturing and the trend is growing in both the US and UK.

57 per cent of manufacturing companies in the UK are considering changing the roles of managers and supervisors because they are moving to teamworking or a flatter structure.

In the US 50 per cent of Fortune 500 companies have self-managed teams in place and this figure is predicted to rise to 90 per cent by the end of the century.

The process can provide considerable business benefits. Self-managed teams can take on a wide range of 'management responsibilities', including:

For example, an American insurance company, AAL Insurance, recorded the following improvements three years after it introduced self-managed teams:

- production up by 20 per cent
- processing time down by 75 per cent
- quality up by 70–90 per cent
- staff numbers down by 45 per cent

Supervision
- working procedures
- working hours and breaks
- quality
- budgets

Liaison	• contact with other teams • contact with internal and external suppliers
Human resources	• performance appraisals • selection • leadership issues
Administration	• support function

The key issues identified by organizations which have introduced self-managed teams focus on:

Ownership	The concept of self-management should be 'owned' by all members of the team. It cannot be imposed because team members are being asked to take on a great deal of responsibility.
Commitment	The organization, as well as the team members, must be committed to self-management and understand its benefits.
Support	Communication, support and training will be required to help members take on their new responsibilities.
Skills	As well as existing team working skills, self-managed team members need additional training in skills such as team dynamics, group problem solving, goal setting and conflict resolution.
Rewards	Pay structures may need to be amended to reflect new responsibilities.

改

Time   Like Kaizen, the process of self-managed teams takes time to work. Pilot schemes can help both teams and the organization to adjust.

CHECKLIST SUMMARY

- 'Leadership' is the art of being consciously responsive to the requirements of the task, the team and the individuals within the team. In that tasks change and the needs of people at work change too, the different skills of leadership must be practiced flexibly with due regard to operational and human demands.

- Kaizen team leaders recognize the primacy of their human relationship skills over craft or technical skills. Their responsibilities as coach, counsellor, educator, trainer, motivator and team manager differentiate them from traditional supervisors, who can be more responsive to and driven by quantitative outputs than the quality of processes, relationships and the working environment.

- A leader who is self-confident, confident in his or her team and capable of managing the team consensually should be able to delegate much command and control to the team itself, thus encouraging a self-directed, or a leaderless, team. This will enable the leader to develop their role as a boundary manager, managing by exception, and to plan the assignment of short- and long-term roles to goals with regard to individuals' competencies and needs.

- Such factors as 'ownership', 'sharing', self-management', 'consensus management' and 'close intra-team liaison' characterize Kaizen teams and, by direct implication, the role of Kaizen team leaders.

8

TRAINING

改善

---

*Training should not be regarded as an isolated
activity, separated from day-to-day working*

Western organizations have tended to treat training as the solution to poor performance, in other words training is what you get when you are doing something wrong. This approach has not raised motivation levels towards training, and managers seem to feel that if they had managed to employ the best people training would not be necessary at all.

---

*Quality starts with education and ends with
education (JUSE)*

The traditional Japanese approach is very different, largely because of the cultural and education differences, and, even though the Japanese education system is currently subject to criticism and change, it is worth exploring these differences more fully. Japanese companies have traditionally built on the strengths of Japanese society which displays characteristics such as commitment, dedication, loyalty, competence, respect, mutual aid and a striving for improvement.

The Japanese education system reinforces these characteristics by:

- encouraging individuals to:
    - learn facts – follow instructions – work hard – strive for high achievement
- enhancing social behaviour
- focusing on generalist rather than specific skills
- regarding further education as a social, rather than an educational, process
- stressing the importance of the 'best' school or university
- featuring a tough recruitment system
- tending to produce graduates without specific skills but who have been trained to learn.

Once a recruit becomes an employee, corporate training further encourages diligence as well as the attitude that the benefit of the organization is the recruit's ultimate goal.

Recruitment is for an organization not for a specific job

Although the situation is beginning to change, recruits in Japan join an organization straight after school or university and hope to stay within it for the whole of their working life. Management training courses outside the companies themselves are rare in Japan and although some Japanese study for MBAs in Europe or the US, their main purpose is to assess Western ways and make contacts (Making Buddies in America?) rather than absorb skills.

Most recruits do not know which department they will work in first, until initial training is complete and staff get to know the recruits and assess their character as well as their skills.

There are two basic training routes – one for graduates and one for school leavers.

INTERNAL TRAINING ENSURES CONTINUITY

External trainers are rarely used; this means that experience and advice can be passed down directly through internally-produced training manuals, with superiors acting as trainers and colleagues sharing their knowledge with each other.

Managers switch readily between management and training. The training and development of employees is an integral part of a manager's job description. In an environment characterized by lifetime employment and promotion based on seniority, senior employees do not feel threatened by younger employees to whom they impart knowledge and experience.

Manuals as a training vehicle

Typically these manuals not only indicate how to perform specific procedures, they also describe how to behave in order to create a good working atmosphere and a peaceful and co-operative organization.

They cover extremely high levels of detail, including suitable workwear, how deeply to bow, how to answer the telephone and where to sit in a car, train or meeting with colleagues.

Most important, the manuals, in common with all other forms of training, stress the organization's philosophy. Through lecture courses, training manuals and personal encouragement, recruits are guided towards:

- paying attention to minute detail
- striving for perfection
- performing to the best of their ability within their particular job
- achieving close communication with colleagues.

改

SPECIFIC TRAINING ACTIVITIES

These include:

Quality Control Circles where employees are trained to be 'quality people', constantly inspecting and checking for defects or mistakes. Within this type of scheme, there is no question of blaming people for specific defects; the emphasis is on the process of achieving the highest quality possible.

Suggestion schemes and **quality control initiatives** which may in some cases be compulsory and in others voluntary. Any suggestions are welcomed from any employee and many are backed by financial rewards. In recent years, to reduce the number of totally impractical ideas, there has been a trend to encourage people to try out their ideas and only put forward those that work in practice.

Job rotation ensures that employees develop a wide range of skills by moving from one job or another. Specialist skills are not uncommon, particularly in scientific positions, but it is more likely that staff will be specialists in a variety of functions. Job rotation can take the form of temporary transfer, but more often is based on a series of two or three year stays in different departments or different jobs before a specialist area is chosen.

Although reward is generally based on seniority, salary levels are sometimes linked to skills. At Toshiba, for example, multi-skilled employees earn a bonus, depending on how many skills they have acquired.

Study clubs and cultural classes

Employees are encouraged to attend in-house classes, with the mutual support of their colleagues, to improve their personal skills and therefore their contribution to the organization

Induction and post induction training

As already discussed, induction in Japan is a comparatively lengthy process and it may be only after several months of training that recruits will work on their own. Post induction off-the-job training is widely used and most organizations have a schedule such as the one below for potential managers.

Year One	Seminars to generate interest in the organization.	10–13 days
Year Two	Seminars to encourage loyalty and increase understanding.	3 days
Year Three	Seminars to demonstrate how to deal effectively with customers.	6 days
Year Four	Seminars to deepen understanding of corporate image and refine ability to handle customers.	3 days

Off the job training

At the Kintetsu department store, employees are encouraged to learn something new every day

Most large organizations have their own training centre, staffed by company employees, but sometimes visited by external trainers or consultants.

The courses utilize simulations, lectures, seminars and other group activities. Skills training will again reinforce the organization's philosophy and show how it can be applied to learning.

THE MANAGER AS INSTRUCTOR

One of a Japanese manager's most important roles is to develop their employees. As most managers will have spent considerable time in different departments and roles, they will have a clear grasp of the problems of younger employees and they can speak with credibility on the subjects and problems they face.

The training role helps to make the manager/employee relationship a close one. Physically, most teams work in close proximity; in an office, for example, the team may sit around a bank of desks with no private rooms or partitioning screens. Employees new to a department can pick up a lot just by listening and observing.

Most managers go further. They or colleagues who are in the same age group as the new recruit will spend a considerable amount of time explaining work and background, writing explanatory notes or encouraging the employee to record their own notes. Managers will include recruits in many meetings, so they can learn by observation and taking notes before they are able to contribute.

The principle is that managers will also generally take an interest in the overall welfare of their employees and will try to be helpful when personal problems arise. As employees are valued for what they contribute personally, it is important that they are not worried by problems at home or work that can be overcome.

EXAMPLES OF JAPANESE TRAINING PROGRAMMES

SENSHU ELECTRONICS (cable manufacturers)

Formal induction training of 11 days for all new recruits at the company training centre.

All subsequent training is on the job. On average, one day is spent observing a new procedure, another observing, practising and taking advice. Subsequent training takes the form of 'rescue' advice. Once a month, the president addresses the whole organization.

FUJITSU (computer manufacturers)

Recruits from top universities join either the design or manufacturing division, where they spend two to three years designing computers and a similar period producing them. Employees are unlikely to spend more than five years in any job before they are considered 'burnt out' and rotated into another role.

TOYOTA (vehicle manufacturer)

The Toyota training programme encourages employees to think in terms of the three C's – be Creative, take Challenges and have Courage – throughout their period of lifetime employment. Education and training programmes aim to enhance the capability and raise the motivation of all employees.

From an early stage, trainees undertake important duties: they are encouraged by their superiors to realize the importance of their roles and to learn by trial and error.

Senior managers are involved in the training and development process, visiting sites, giving advice and guidance and participating in voluntary training and development activities such as those of the Toyota Club.

Strengths and weaknesses of the Japanese approach

Strengths

- co-operation and strong common purpose
- close relationship between managers and team members; better communication
- multiskilling and rotation means a flexible workforce, few interdepartmental barriers, stronger networks and better overall understanding
- all managers are experienced and can speak with understanding

改

- atmosphere of trust, esteem and confidence
- high average level of competence and commitment.

Weaknesses

- some lack of critical analysis
- some lack of creativity and individual innovation
- lack of specialization can mean lack of professionalism in some areas
- not so exciting for young people or (traditionally) for women
- very time-consuming because of continuous training and job rotation.

ACHIEVING THE BEST OF EAST AND WEST

Clearly, the cultural, social and behavioural differences between Japan and the West mean that it would be impossible to transfer Japanese methods as they stand. However, as the following table shows, both Japanese and Western approaches have positive aspects and both groups can learn from each other.

Western training approach	*Japanese training approach*
Emphasis on external training	Few business schools, mostly in-house, on-the-job training
Training in one department	Training in a variety of departments
Specialist career progression	Generalist career progression
Managers young, sometimes less experienced than staff	Managers rarely under 30
Managers tend to be remote from staff, act as leaders	Managers are part of team, understand staff problems and have close relationships
Look at the work performance of employees	Consider the whole person's development and performance

Bring in outside trainers and motivators	Motivate through building up team spirit
Appraisal systems to evaluate training	Few formal appraisals, frequent informal discussions
Training department reports to personnel department	Training department reports direct to senior management
Judged by financial status	Take a long-term view of profit and personal progress

While the Japanese approach has failings, particularly in the fostering of creativity and individual approaches, the Western approach has in the past also been only partly successful. The school system has given generalist, grounding education to children up to the age of eleven when they change schools and, particularly in the UK, begin to specialize from that age. Any child who does not do well at school by the age of eleven is encouraged towards a more practical education and academically gifted children are encouraged to specialize in either arts or sciences, using their test and exam results as the only criteria. This has resulted in some scientists and technical staff at work being uncomfortable with writing and communications skills while an artistic graduate may have difficulties with mathematics and budgeting.

Although many children undertake some form of vocational training it is generally geared towards a specific career but certainly by the time the majority join organizations they consider their training is behind them.

The same has been true of senior management who have tended to ridicule the idea of any further, including management, training believing that experience is the best teacher. There is, of course, a great deal in this maxim but sadly many senior management appeared to learn little from their experiences and their constant refrain is 'I don't need any training – I've been doing it for years perfectly well'.

In the past this system may have led to a highly-skilled specialist workforce, but in the current climate of rapidly increasing change, it is not providing the flexible, willing to learn and change employees that an organization needs for its survival.

The Management Development to the Millennium report produced by the British Institute of Management identified from a survey of its members that the key skills required for the year 2001 would be:

- strategic thinking
- responding to and managing change
- orientation to total quality/customer satisfaction
- financial management
- facilitating others to contribute
- understanding the role of information and IT
- verbal communication
- organizational sensitivity
- risk assessment in decision making.

It is interesting to note that the majority of these skills are of the 'softer' variety rather than the work-based skills that have previously been encouraged.

The report also highlighted the methods it identified as being most relevant and appropriate to develop managers for the millennium:

- external courses
- job rotation within organization
- on-the-job training programme
- internal courses
- project work
- self-managed learning.

Members contributing to the survey interestingly identify that they need additional training and development to be ready to face the challenges of the millennium and that they see a variety of ways previously uncommon in the West to achieve it.

At a conference held recently sponsored by the International Productivity Service (made up of government representatives from USA, Canada, Europe, Asia and the Tokyo-based Global Industrial and Social Progress Research Institute) similar concerns were raised. It was acknowledged that Western training methods had not provided all that could be desired. One US official said 'we produce people who are highly skilled on the computer but who don't have the ability to compose a letter on it'.

They called for strategic alliances with schools to provide more broadly competent graduates and linked on-the-job training to the ability of the Japanese to produce highly-skilled and flexible employees. The US view was that the West was giving far too much information early on in an employee's career when there was little opportunity to utilize it. On-the-job training tells people just what they need to know at the moment they need to use it.

Some organizations are making strides to resolve their training concerns.

EASTMAN CHEMICAL COMPANY

Eastman Chemical Company based in Tennessee USA, decided in 1991 to move from a function-orientated organization to a market-driven company focused on product lines. Its reorganization strategy included a major companywide policy entitled 'Education and training: encourage learning and personal growth for everyone throughout their careers'. The company set up a project team of salespeople, trainers, employees from the business units and other employees with very strong management support to create a mission.

It then established a training programme made up of all the

▶

competencies that were required for each group of jobs and various training options to meet them. These competencies are now being used by employees for career planning. The training options fell into four categories:

- in-house training sessions
- self-directed courses
- literature (other than internal training materials)
- external courses, seminars and conferences.

Employees could choose the topics and learning methods that suited them best (thus recognizing that each individual learns best in different ways) and also decide their availability for training.

A project team member visited the senior management at each site and helped launch the project to the employees as well as producing a Training Process Manual that included a message from the CEO stressing the importance of the project.

After four months, a survey showed that 70 per cent of respondents had used the process and were mostly satisfied. The project team is still working to provide training for employees:

- at all locations
- in employees' first language
- that is culturally appropriate
- that links international employees.

British organizations are responding in many different ways to the challenge of training for the management and staff of the future. In the past, training has been seen as a very expensive process with no guarantee of a long-term benefit. When MBAs first became popular in the 1980s, many organizations found that as soon as they had paid the final bills and welcomed their newly-qualified member of staff back into the fold this member of staff was poached by a competitor who got all the benefits of the expensive training in return for a high salary.

Between the 1950s and 1980s the BBC had a reputation for

training the television crews of the world. It had the resources to take in young school leavers and graduates, train them superbly well and in enough quantity to allow a large proportion of them to be poached by national and international competitors. These days, as the pool of BBC technicians, and therefore the number of trainees, has fallen, the poaching companies are having to set up their own training schemes.

So, how can an organization retain its expensively trained staff?

The answer is not a simple one. While some organizations do not invest in their own training, an element will always be poached for higher salaries elsewhere. The only conclusion seems to be to take the longer view. If you want your staff to be well-trained and developed, your organization will need to make the investment and trust that if your strategies are correct and that the staff feel a sense of involvement and on-going support and development, a sense of loyalty is likely to be engendered and you will only lose a few. Other organizations have prided themselves on the the fact that the brightest and best in their industry started in their training scheme and therefore they will be attracting the cream of the young crop wishing to join. But it is certainly an issue that the HR department need to consider during their strategy sessions.

One sign that training in softer skills is taking root in the UK is the increasing number of organizations seeking Investor in People accreditation. Investors in People (IIP) funded originally through the Department of Employment and implemented through the Training and Enterprise Councils (TECs) has set itself ambitious targets of 50 per cent of companies with more than 200 employees recognized by 1996. Whether it will achieve its aims or not, is not yet clear; it is interesting that only 44 per cent of a recent sample of companies not involved in it, had heard of it. Again, it seems to be, yet again, that genuine commitment is lacking from senior management and those that are

改

interested may have different motives. It is clear that the recognition 'Award' is a business advantage and that some organizations have found it very valuable, although others have found it too lengthy a process. Kaizen training fits well as an addition to IIP, as several Europe Japan Centre clients have discovered; it provides the structures to make sure the improvements made during the IIP process continue to bear fruit in the future.

What training in the West needs is genuine commitment to both skills training and the personal development of all its staff. Too much of a focus on task-based qualifications, useful as they are in developing quality and confidence, leads inevitably to a narrow specialized workforce. To balance the process qualities, it is important to invest equally in the 'life' skills of communication, listening, people management and facilitation.

POLYGRAM

Polygram, the London-based entertainment company, is committed to developing its staff and believes that 'a learning organization is one that teaches itself'. It has found that training seems to mean much more to those undergoing it, if it refers particularly to what they are doing. Managers run seminars for each other, for example on financial and commercial subjects, rather than booking external courses. Not only is this form of internal training completely relevant to the organization and the individuals concerned, but it saves both time and money in comparison to external training. Polygram have also discovered 'that we've got several financial people who are brilliant teachers'. The time cost of the in-house expert can be balanced against the advantages of relationship building that occurs in the process.

How this training will be delivered is an area that is attracting more and more attention.

The move towards more in-company designed and delivered

training is setting a major challenge to both business schools and other training establishments. Many of them, including outdoor activity centres, are now meeting with their clients to design and build genuinely individually tailored programmes to meet the particular needs of the organization. In the past 'individually tailored programmes' have tended to mean a training company lifting the modules required from their files and making small adaptions to fit the requirements. Organizations are now demanding a better service from their training suppliers and rightly working in partnership to ensure that they get and pay for what they want. There has been a perceptible shift in power from a training consultancy telling organizations what they need, to a partnership between supplier and customer.

Other organizations are now creating powerful learning establishments of their own.

MERVYN

Mervyn's retail chain in San Francisco has gone so far as to create its own university with all the US collegiate trappings, next door to its corporate headquarters. Here managers come together to experience 'the turning points of their lives'. One module, The Area Manager in Training programme, consists of ten weeks of classroom instruction and on-the-job training in an actual store run by a manager whose performance and experience are regarded as exceptional. Exams and tests are set at regular intervals and participants must pass before moving onto the next phase. Emotions can run high as trainees realize the risks of failing but this seems to engender a strong sense of partnership within them.

There are plans to increase the number of universities within the organization and increase the number of programmes. Mervyn's point to the tremendous increase in the skill level of new managers, an improved hiring profile, and a noticeable difference in a department run by one of the graduates as tangible proof of success.

UNIPART

Unipart, the British car part manufacturer, also has its own in-house 'university' known as Unipart 'U' where the Managing Director and many other managers are involved in developing and delivering training. Expert outside lecturers, including a team from the British Government's Treasury department, visit to speak and a library is open to all staff. Courses are available on IT, customer service, introductory programmes for new employees and personal development programmes ranging from time management to a certificate in management. In the first six months of the 'U', many staff achieved as many as ten days training each.

As far as the designers of the 'U' are concerned, it is achieving many of the things they set out as goals and, with management deeply involved, has been a catalyst in changing thinking about training.

HARVESTER RESTAURANTS

Harvester Restaurants are an example of organizations attempting to match the spirit of what they are developing to the style in which it is delivered. It awards study tours to observe and experience 'hospitality' as practised by other leisure organizations. Recently it has sent team managers on a study tour to Florida to research and experience Disney's management organization and style.

Training and development plans are rapidly spreading to organizations in the service sectors and to professions, as well as to smaller organizations, where management skills were not traditionally highly valued.

One example is **Clewley & Co.** a Chartered Accounting practice based in the Telford area, UK. The company is 'prepared to take people with the right attitude and helps them develop, even though they may not have come to accountancy through a formally recognized route'. Their training and development activities include:

- a personal training plan for each staff member
- a monthly training session for all staff on management and communication skills
- a long-term training plan for the practice, reviewed every six months
- training courses, tailored to specific needs, including information technology, counselling skills and driving lessons
- distance learning for trainees in accounting qualifications with regular supervision and discussion of progress
- monthly staff meeting to review the performance of the practice.

MEASURING TRAINING EFFECTIVENESS

Measuring training in levels of knowledge and skills as a result of training can be done relatively easily via tests of pre- and post-training levels. A more complex task is evaluating training which aims to change attitudes and behaviour. Statistics may be useful in certain cases: poor morale, for example, is frequently reflected in high rates of absenteeism, stoppages, accidents, staff turnover, disciplinary actions etc, all of which can, and in a Kaizen organization should, be measured.

Conversely, factors associated with Kaizen-type organizations typically contribute to low rates of absenteeism, turnover etc.

At **Boots the Chemist**, in the UK, for example, low absence rates are considered to be encouraged by:

- small teams of four to five employees
- close supervision in stores
- an attractive, bright workplace

▶

▶
> ● contact with the public, which keep interest levels high
> ● staff are made to feel they make a personal contribution to business and are kept well-informed through briefings.

Other techniques include questionnaires asking participants to give their views, for example, on attitudes which support Kaizen, at the beginning of a training session and at the end. Scales can be used to measure shifts:

A 'Kaizen person' ...	Agree strongly			Disagree strongly	
pays attention to detail	1	2	3	4	5
is co-operative	1	2	3	4	5
works well in teams	1	2	3	4	5
is forward-looking	1	2	3	4	5

Peer opinions may also be asked – providing this is done in a no-blame atmosphere – in order to assess the extent to which a person may exhibit, for example, Kaizen attitudes before and after a training course.

INTEGRATED TRAINING

Although training may be useful in developing the knowledge, skills, or attitudes of an individual participant, it is all too easy for these advances to be lost once the participant returns to their daily work. Various methods can be used to try and 'embed' the training:

● ask the participant to give other team members a summary of the training, or to pick out one or two specific points which other people could benefit from

- make sure the manager/team leader hears about the results of the training and tries to make opportunities for the participant to practice the new skills
- montior whether the new attitudes or skills are used when they are needed, and if not, investigate the reasons and explore the need for further training.

改大

CHECKLIST SUMMARY

To paraphrase, the Management Development to the Millennium concludes that there are six key challenges facing management with numbers 1, 3 and 6 identified as priorities:

1 Organizations, both large and small, need to be educated to recognize that investment in development contributes directly to long-term competitiveness.

2 Managers and staff must commit themselves to life-long learning.

3 Senior management must provide commitment and leadership.

4 Standards and qualifications must be transferrable and widely acceptable.

5 Providers must recognize and respond to the diverse training and development needs of users.

6 A more coherent infrastructure for management and staff development must be created.

Additionally:

- balance the credibility of task-skills qualifications with the personal development of softer, people-based skills

- consider how most effectively to deliver this training and tailor it to the individual rather than just the organization

- when setting the HR strategy, consider how you intend to respond to the challenge of retaining expensively-trained staff.

9

DEVELOPMENT

TRAINING AND DEVELOPMENT

For the purposes of clarification, this book considers training to be the acquisition of knowledge that is required for the job while development is the acquisition of knowledge that is of value to the individual concerned but may have no direct relevance to either their current or even future jobs.

One of the reasons that personal development of the individual is now being considered by organizations is to help create the flexible, involved and willing-to-embrace-change employees that so many organizations have found difficulty in recruiting.

Professor Charles Handy of the London Business School has estimated that human beings fulfil less than 20 per cent of their true potential; some philosophy teachers in the East have suggested that the figure is even lower. One thing is clear: nearly all employees have considerably more to offer their organization and society than at present is being tapped. Tom Peters, the American business author, suggests that if organizations could see all the things their employees achieved outside of their working lives, they would be amazed at how capable they are. The question for Western organizations is how to tap this huge potential resource?

One aspect of personal development that has grown in popularity and proved to be successful in the West is that of coaching, often associated with the mentoring arrangements discussed previously. Rather than giving advice and telling people

改

what to do about work situations, a positive step to helping them develop confidence and take more responsibility for their own development is to rephrase the question back to them. So when a member of staff says 'What should I do about this problem?', the coach is likely to say 'Yes, I can see that it is a problem, what options do you think you have?'

Through this type of process the employee is encouraged to take responsibility, identify possible solutions and further training needs rather than it being imposed from above. Encouraging employees to take responsibility for their own career and personal development leads to a high degree of motivation and commitment.

HARVESTER RESTAURANTS' COACHING PROGRAMME

Harvester, the UK restaurant chain, has implemented teamworking throughout its organization and each team is expected to act as a continuous learning group. To facilitate this, Harvester has assigned to each team a coach who plays a very important part in employee development. The task of the coach is to give the support, advice, training and development necessary to enable the team to fulfil its role as well as put into practice the concept of continuous development. Each coach is carefully selected and trained for his or her work and has continual close support from Harvester's central training team.

In the past few years several organizations in the West have successfully launched personal development programmes and have discovered that whatever learning an employee embarks on, even outside the workplace for their own satisfaction, has potential benefits for the organization. Staff learning languages for their holidays are obviously developing a skill that might have a work-related benefit. But what about evening classes in DIY or embroidery?

Their experience is that any learning at all has positive benefits for the individual including:

- enhanced confidence and self-esteem
- attraction to other sorts of learning (eg skills)
- a flexibility of mind which encourages flexibility of attitude
- increased willingness to embrace change,

all of which have enormous benefits to their organization.

How can an organization encourage continual personal development amongst its employees? In Britain there is already in place a substantial infrastructure of opportunities in the community:

- libraries
- evening classes
- the Open University available to anyone with access to a television.

Many organizations are now including information about ongoing education on their staff bulletin boards.

If we take a hypothetical example, during an appraisal (*See* next chapter) a manager or coach might discover that a member of staff is dissatisfied with their current position and encourage them to, say, study for an Open University MBA, even if they might leave the organization when completed. Because of the manager's support and encouragement, it is likely that the employee will be remotivated at work.

Many organizations' social clubs have additional benefits of team building together with the focus of the club which may include:

- sports
- fitness classes
- theatre trips
- art gallery trips.

The examples of organizational support quoted above cost little, if anything, for the organization and very likely they have not been conscious of the development benefits they are reaping. Most social club activities, for example, are organized in an individual's own time whilst the organization gives only passive encouragement.

One aspect to personal development that is growing rapidly in the UK is the use of Personal Development Plans (PDPs). In some organizations these take the form of a personal file that the employee keeps and fills in on a regular basis before using it as the basis of part of the appraisal process (*See* next chapter). In other organizations, these are now being incorporated into software which helps ensure that they are more immediately available than a hard copy file which may be out of sight, and therefore out of mind. Any form of file has the advantage of making the process rather more structured and therefore more likely to be followed. The paperwork or software programme can ensure that it is clear that the organization is committed to it and because the manager will see it on a regular basis, that they are involved in a support role. The programme or paperwork can set out a formal process so that each topic can be graded and therefore reviewed more effectively. For example:

Skill	Making presentations
Present level	2 (personal assessment – out of 5)
Target level	3 (by September)
Actions identified	attending one-day course in May social club AGM June presentation to management August
Further action	look for more practice opportunities June–August

Setting targets and actions to achieve them are vital parts of any development programmes. Some form of measurement is helpful to see progress and build confidence.

It may be helpful to consider some of the proactive approaches to personal development that different organizations have taken.

FORD'S EMPLOYEE DEVELOPMENT AND ASSISTANCE PROGRAMME

Ford UK launched its EDAP in line with its holistic approach strategy and sees it as part of its 'broad, humanist' attitude. The programme is non-job related and its purpose is to 'empower' its staff. Grants support employees on courses as varied as losing weight, stopping smoking, 27 foreign languages, underwater photography etc. Each employee has an allowance of up to £200 for non-vocational training of their choice and 30,000 UK employees have already taken part.

CALVERT

Calvert, a US mutual fund investment group, has committed in its mission to 'preserving quality of life' and has pioneered socially responsible investment. In line with these values it rewards employees who walk to work by buying them training shoes (as well as protecting the environment, it promotes fitness) and pays employees for up to 12 days a year community service (allowing them to pursue personal interests while giving back to the community). The company's tuition reimbursement programme allows workers to collect up to £3,000 a year for whatever type of learning they choose and courses have varied from basket-weaving to classes towards a law degree. Evelyn Steward, vice president of human resources, says 'It's the employees who make the company successful, so we put a lot of focus on doing what we can for the workforce'.

Action: Employees in the Community (in partnership with Business in the Community) encourages businesses to set up employee volunteering and secondment programmes and in 1994/5 a record 9000 employees were involved. According to recent figures (Charities Aid Foundation 1995) one-third of large companies in the UK currently support employees to get involved in community activities outside the workplace. (The figure in the US is 91 per cent according to the Conference Board in 1993.) The Institute of Management members polled (Coe 1994) on the main benefits to the organization of involvement in voluntary work identified:

Public relations	69%
Staff development	68%
Management development	48%
Staff morale	33%
Breaks down barriers	30%
Business contacts	25%

In a recent evaluation 52 individuals from seven participating organizations (including Nationwide Building Society and Marks and Spencer) assessed themselves on their improvement in thirteen competencies during their community activity:

Collaboration	72%
Communication	68%
Influencing skills	68%
Customer focus	63%
Adaptability	62%
Leadership	62%
Decisiveness	58%
Creative Thinking/Innovation	58%
Project management skills	55%
Excellence/continuous improvement	55%

Technical/professional skills	55%
Business awareness	52%
Maximize performance	48%

The respondents were asked whether their own performance back at work had been enhanced. 78 per cent said it had and 56 per cent said the overall performance of their company had been enhanced as a result.

Community involvement is likely to be a growing trend in small as well as large organizations for both its PR and morale benefits as well as its undoubted results in the personal development of staff.

HOW ROVER HAS ADOPTED THE TOTAL APPROACH TO LEARNING

The Rover Learning Business (part of Rover Cars) represents a radical new approach to training. It claims not to offer training in the conventional sense but instead to offer opportunities to learn job skills as well as other skills that are useful to employees beyond the workplace. The aim is to benefit both the employee's sense of personal fulfilment and Rover Group profitability. This approach aims to get training away from something that is imposed by management to something the employees want to do for themselves.

As well as conventional job-related skills training, Rover also offers employees a selection of courses as diverse as brick-laying, ballroom dancing and pottery.

According to Rover, 'It's been recognized that greater competitiveness in business cannot be achieved by management alone. Some means had to be found to energize every employee to harness their talents towards a common purpose – hence the arrival of the Rover Learning Business.'

To communicate its purpose to the whole of the Rover Group, RLB has set out its aims in a mission statement:

▶

改

'RLB is committed to being the market leader in providing continuous learning and development for all employees. The environment will motivate and enable individuals to make the most of opportunities provided for individual achievement as well as support for continued growth of the Rover Group, its suppliers and the francise dealer network'.

RLB's objectives are also clearly stated:

- provide top-quality training and development service to all employees of Rover, its dealerships and suppliers regardless of geography and with equality of opportunity
- develop line managers so that they act as facilitators of the learning process
- develop a range of products and infrastructure to implement a method known as the Personal Development File and create new learning opportunities
- support integration and accelerate change through application of Rover's Corporate Learning Process
- create genuine growth in customer demand – and be seen as the preferred supplier
- encourage a common thread and consistency of purpose in learning activities
- utilize appropriate technology
- operate through a flexible team structure
- attract external funding
- enhance the performance of Rover dealerships worldwide
- support Rover's tactical commercial activities
- produce customer researched, integrated and piloted programmes.

Some aspects of the learning programme were compulsory – training of all employees to ensure Total Quality Management – however 88000 voluntary training days in one year were shared by the workforce – an indication to Rover of the untapped potential to employee development, and the enthusiasm of employees for personal development.

To ensure that the programme developed in the right direction, the company carried out an extensive survey among employees:

- all 35,000 employees received a letter from the MD telling them how important learning would be
- 4,000 employees received a survey seeking their views on the learning process and more than 75 per cent responded

The key findings of the survey were:

- need for better awareness of existing learning opportunities
- more positive support from the line manager
- greater recognition from the company for individual achievement.

The programmes were introduced to staff through an audio tape and a workbook which explained the process and benefits of learning. It stresses that learning is an individual process – hence the variety of techniques used by RLB – and that learning will be adapted to the individual.

The introduction also stresses Rover's commitment to its people, in order to:

- distinguish the group as the best in Europe for attracting, retaining and developing people
- emphasize the view that people are the company's greatest asset
- gain recognition by employees that the company's commitment to every individual has increased
- unlock and recognize employee's talents and make better use of those talents
- gain recognition and a seal of approval for employee achievements through internal and external accrediting bodies.

Employees are involved in the development of their own future. The Personal Development File gives an employee an opportunity to plan an individual development programme using previous experience and self-assessment. People obtain tangible evidence of their own development and their competencies can be integrated with a career promotion structure.

RLB has the commitment of the line management team to support the programme:

- line managers helped to develop the programme
- many of the programmes are led by line managers
- the RLB professionals support the line managers and help them to deliver the programmes.

RLB works with associates in each of the functional departments who are responsible for local learning output. They are involved in preparation of material for new product launches.

RLB supports the line managers in their new role by:

- detailed briefing on their responsibilities before the process began
- specific training to help them identify potential and build enthusiasm for the learning process
- a management development programme offering managers a range of opportunities to improve their capability, including project management, coaching and self-development

Rover pays for all job-related training and, additionally, pays up to £100 per year through Rover Employees Assisted Learning scheme for learning that is not directly relevant to the job. They believe that the additional learning helps self esteem and encourages a positive attitude to learning.

To match the RLB resources to individual learning requirements, the company uses a variety of internal and external resources and, in some cases, develops customized courses for particular requirements.

RLB also aims to make training more accessible:

- courses that might have been provided through night school are now provided at the end of shifts and thus minimize the inconvenience for employees

- distance learning is used so that employees can learn in their own time.

The learning process can demonstrate considerable cost benefits to senior management:

- corporate learning process, through which improvements to cost management, yielded cost avoidance/savings of millions of pounds per annum
- learning also contributed to lead time reduction of vehicle supply
- the introduction of TQM into the supplier chain also contributes to better overall corporate performance.

CHECKLIST SUMMARY

Japanese corporate training at its best encourages the personal commitment, attention to detail, dedication to improvement, team spirit and other human factors that have been such key factors in Japanese business success. While Japanese companies are now looking for new ideas to help them succeed in the 21st century, there are still many Western organizations that are not placing sufficient emphasis on the human factor in training and development and are, therefore, failing to achieve their full potential.

Those organizations that, through continuous training and development, are able to harness the commitment of their employees, as well as creating a climate of creativity and excitement, will be well-placed to lead their sector, not only in Europe or the US, but worldwide.

These are some of the key characteristics that could be adapted from Japanese companies:

- rotation and multiskilling

- more emphasis on company philosophy, vision and mission to build higher levels of commitment

- review the role of the manager as instructor

- concentrate on motivation through team building

- introduce a culture of continuous improvement in staff development as well as production/service techniques

- take a longer-term view of personal progress, rather than measuring progress against financial targets

- listen to employees' ideas and suggestions

- meet the needs and tap the creativity of every employee.

10

APPRAISALS

改善

From research that the Europe Japan Centre has undertaken it is clear that, despite large-scale changes among Western organizations (with the development of flatter structures intended to encourage a more flexible and enabled workforce working together more cohesively with a greater reliance on personal responsibility, self motivation and self management), there has been little change in the approach to appraisals. People's attitudes and expectations about their working lives have also changed as they realize the need to be more flexible in a rapidly changing world and in the climate of down-sizing. Employees more often than not want to make a greater contribution but often feel stifled through there being too few appropriate channels in place to develop ideas.

It is often the case that even in organizations seeking to develop quality people, the traditional appraisal system linking pay to performance may actually act as a deterrent. It will not necessarily help the organization work towards its goals in quality and it may even demotivate staff and so undo progress achieved in other areas.

THE TRADITIONAL APPROACH TO APPRAISALS

- centrally-devised and run by the personnel department
- aims to assess and compare employees across the board
- uses standard report format and rating scales
- too often acts as a basis for distribution of pay
- is often carried out by a supervisor with limited knowledge of the appraisal process
- limited knowledge of the person being appraised
- limited scope for development and improvement.

The Europe Japan Centre often hears responses to these traditional approaches to appraisal, in the following terms:

'Oh no, it's that time of year again'

'My boss doesn't see me from one week to the next. How can he possibly judge my performance?'

'It's a joke, they haven't yet done any of the things we agreed on last year.'

In Britain, in particular, people often shy away first from celebrating achievement and second giving constructive feedback. The following scenario may seem a little far fetched, but in reality is close to the experiences of thousands of appraisees in many different organizations.

A TYPICAL APPRAISAL

The meeting opens with both the appraisor and appraisee rather embarrassedly acknowledging a few successes and achievements. Both then move on towards the next phase of the appraisal as quickly as possible without any form of analysis of *how* the success was achieved. Then in 'areas of improvement', the appraisor, who probably at this point is uncomfortable with giving feedback on behaviour and events that have spanned the last year, takes the bull by the horns and issues a whole catalogue of things that could have been better. At this, the appraisee sits back with glazed eyes, convinced that their whole year has been disastrous.

These traditional approaches tend to evoke feelings of fear and dread, and many people regard them as unfair, one-sided, irrelevant and bureaucratic because they:

- promote a 'them and us' attitude
- foster secrecy and a closed culture
- tend to be largely negative and demotivating
- can undermine teamworking and be divisive
- do little to promote empowerment.

None of these aspects will be acceptable to organizations which are striving to develop their people.

THE NEED FOR A NEW APPROACH

There is a need for a new form of appraisal that takes the developmental approach

An organization that is committed, through its people, to achieving the highest levels of customer satisfaction, the flexibility to respond to changing market needs, innovative and high-quality products and high-levels of productivity will need to reappraise its own appraisal system.

The first point to consider is the complete removal of the element of financial reward from the process and to this end, this book will remove the topic from this chapter and give it one of its own (next chapter).

Dr Deming suggests that appraisal systems in their own right are irrelevant. Good managers should know their staff well, be continually aware of how they are performing and show an on-going commitment to their development rather than considering it just once yearly. There is a great deal of common sense in his view, but to organizations which are loath to throw out the baby with the bathwater it may be encouraging to consider that, in addition to regular communication, a yearly review of some sort is often helpful. All human beings tend to benefit from looking back at their past achievements and planning their future, whether this be on New Year's Eve or on their birthday.

A Kaizen organization's review or appraisal system might be seen to support the following:

- high-quality, educated and well-informed staff
- continuous improvement of people
- empowered employees
- respect for the individual
- co-operation and teamwork
- supportive, hands-off management
- flat structures
- open communications with two-way information flow
- cross-functional working with a new role to:
- help employees do their present work better and create an environment of continuous improvement
- help employees develop so that they can undertake wider, different roles or enjoy and perform their current one more effectively.

DEVELOPING NEW PROCESSES AND FRAMEWORKS

Organizations have different cultures and structures and no single appraisal or review system will be suitable for them all.

Each organization needs to develop its own framework and processes. It is, however, possible to identify a number of fundamental principles for effective systems, including:

- who should be involved in the process
- the indicators that should be used
- the style of management essential to support the process.

Principles of a developmental attitude

- human factors not financial targets
- link to business needs
- run by team leaders or line managers
- open
- participative
- an integrated approach
- single status
- adaptable
- team element
- on-going and informal

Human factors not financial targets

In relating appraisal to development, it is imperative to remove the competitiveness from within an organization and replace it with co-operation (it is, after all, your competitor you should be competing with rather than each other). Co-operation can be strengthened if human factors, rather than financial targets are used as criteria. Appraisals that are linked directly to financial payments or financial rewards tend to induce fear in the individuals and eliminate the opportunity for learning.

Balance quality with quantity

Equally there is a need to restrain the desire to measure everything and assess against these criteria only. Quality has a spirit to it which may not be apparent in the figures you set. One consultant at the Europe Japan Centre in a previous organization found that she had monthly targets for meetings, telephone calls and sales to meet which paid little regard to the volume of the business that might be generated from developing one customer. Meeting targets leads to a focus on 'doing the job right' rather than improving what 'right' is or even whether it is the right thing to be doing at all.

Link to business needs

One of the main reasons for introducing a new form of appraisal process is to improve the organization's performance. It should therefore be closely linked to business needs and balanced with the individual employee's needs.

Run by team leaders or line managers

The process should be owned and driven by line managers or team leaders, who are in daily contact and observe the work of the employee. The personnel department cannot be responsible for giving constructive feedback to a member of staff from other people's written comments.

Open

The process should be open so that the individual involved sees and agrees with what, if anything, is written about them. This should be an on-going developmental process rather than an annual confidential report.

Participative

The process should be participative in two senses:

1 The person being appraised should contribute to the process including significant achievements, development needs and career aspirations.

2 The process should not be dominated by the immediate team leader or manager, and, ideally, should involve inputs from several other sources, for example from other managers, peers, and internal or external customers who have been involved with the individual.

An integrated approach

The appraisal process should not be regarded as a stand-alone activity or operate in a vacuum. It should reinforce the other key elements in the organization's development culture, including pay, rewards, incentives, promotion, job evaluation, training and development.

Single status

The appraisal process should include ALL staff (including management). This will ensure that it becomes part of the culture rather than divisive and aimed at criticizing one level of staff only. It can become a corner-stone of a Kaizen organization, committed to continuously improving its performance and the potential of each of its employees, only if it involves everyone.

Adaptable

It should incorporate procedures for regularly reviewing and updating the process so that it can be changed and adapted as the organization changes and develops. There is no one perfect system for everyone and neither will there be a perfect system for your organization that is appropriate forever.

Team element

When organizations are structured in teams, there should be a strong team element. Objectives should be cascaded to team level, discussed as a team and targets agreed for the team by the team so that individual targets can be agreed in the light of the team targets. A team is only ever as good as each of its members. Therefore no-one's performance stands on its own. An individual's performance is greatly influenced by and should be reviewed by the team itself.

On-going and informal

An ideal appraisal system would be less formal than tradition has dictated, and would take place regularly rather than once or twice a year.

WHO SHOULD BE INVOLVED IN APPRAISALS?

There are several different options available:

- the employee
- peers
- employee, peers and team leader/manager
- managers/team leaders
- upwards appraisal.

The employee

Many appraisal systems remain one-sided and allow the employee only to listen and comment on what the manager says. Good appraisal systems involve employees fully, taking their views into account before and during the appraisal. Self-criticism is a good deal more acceptable than criticism from another and if employees are facilitated to self-evaluate, they are likely to be a great deal more committed to put development projects into action.

Positive aspects

- greater employee commitment to the outcome

- less employee defensiveness
- greater openness about problems
- encourages employees to think about their own performance and development needs in a constructive way
- leads to a more objective assessment.

Negative aspects

- can be taken too far – there is no more value in basing the process exclusively on the employee's view than those of the manager
- risk of obtaining over-lenient staff assessments
- employees may not report accurately on their own behaviour.

Peers

This process is not yet widespread in the UK although it offers a number of important benefits. At Digital Equipment Corporation in the US, employees are appraised by every member of their own self-managed workteam, not just their supervisors.

Typically, the secretary sends electronic mail to the appraisee 30 days before the scheduled time. Appraisees select a Chairperson (usually an advocate of the individual's work) of the Performance Appraisal (PA) committee who nominates a management consultant and two randomly selected team mates. The appraisee prepares his or her own paperwork listing achievements and training and sends it to the committee and the rest of the team. The team then has two weeks to provide input to the Chairperson who collates the information and passes it to the individual concerned. The subject then writes his or her own PA document and sends it to the committee for their review, which takes one week before they meet with the individual concerned, to prepare a development and job plan for the next year.

改

Positive aspects

- very suitable for organizations without formal, hierarchical structures
- peers are often in a position to give a unique insight into an individual's team contribution
- increased participation leads to increased commitment to dealing with the outcome.

Negative aspects

- very time-consuming to collect peer-ratings
- potential to cause friction and disrupt team harmony
- generally, peer rating is not very accurate or unbiased.

Employees, peers and team leader/manager

This is sometimes referred to as 'the 360 degree approach' and is not yet widely used in the UK, although growing rapidly. The National Health Service is using peer assessment of competencies increasingly. In 1980, Gulf Oil adopted this approach on an experimental basis at senior management level. Each manager was invited to choose five to eight people from any level who they believed were qualified to make a valid assessment of their performance. These people were asked to fill in appraisal forms and send them anonymously to the human resources department.

Positive aspects

- more objective, as more people are involved in the process
- more complete picture of employee. This should promote high levels of confidence in the process
- useful where geographical spread or working practices make it hard for a single supervisor to monitor a person's performance effectively.

Negative aspects

- very time consuming
- administratively heavy if more than a small number of people are involved
- some people may need help to learn from this feedback because it may spring some uncomfortable surprises
- can give rise to mutual praise.

Managers/team leaders

Here more than one manager or team leader is involved in the process. For example, a manager is nominated to collect the appraisal information from all the employee's team or project leaders throughout the year and base the appraisal on that.

Positive aspects

- very useful when changes in working practice make it difficult to identify only one person who should conduct the interview.

Negative aspects

- if the employee has no input into whom the nominated 'spokesperson' is, there may be resentment. It is vital that agreement is reached.

Upward appraisal

This system, where team members appraise their team leader, team leaders appraise their managers and so on up the chain, is now becoming more popular in the USA and is creating increasing interest in the UK. Among those already using it are Rank Xerox, BP Exploration, Federal Express, Standard Chartered Bank and American Express.

改

W H Smith, one of Britain's first implementers of upward appraisal, uses it as an additional input to the normal appraisal process for managers. People working for particular managers are asked to fill in questionnaires anonymously, rating their managers on 32 attributes and send the questionnaires to an independent company. The company analyzes the data and prepares a report for each manager which is then used to plan future training and development programmes.

Positive aspects

- facilitates the enablement of employees and the holistic approach to people
- can lead to improved managerial effectiveness, particularly in relation to leadership and people-management by providing a source of direct feedback
- can contribute to a more effective management style which may make the company a more attractive place to work
- avoids possible single rater bias as each manager is now appraised by several team members, not just one manager.

Negative aspects

- very time consuming
- high levels of administration
- managers may feel undermined and react badly
- employees may not be frank enough to make meaningful comments
- employees may use the opportunity to exercise grudges
- employees may fear retaliatory punitive action by managers.

A total bottom-up appraisal system could take the following form:

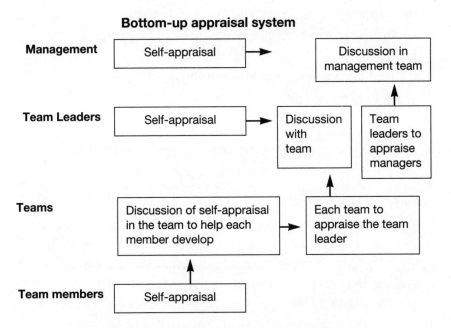

Bottom-up appraisal system

WHAT SHOULD BE ASSESSED?

The change in emphasis to a more developmental approach does not totally remove the need to assess staff in some way. Appraisal that motivates and develops uses two basic indicators:

- achievement against objectives
- achievement in skill and competency acquisition.

Achievement against objectives

- objectives can be set at team or individual level (or both)
- they do not have to be task-related; personal development objectives may also be worth including
- it is vital that objectives are fully discussed and agreed, reviewed and updated regularly.

Achievement in skill and competency acquisition

- employees are assessed against key competencies for their job

- this approach analyzes the progress of the individual and focuses attention on areas where skills can be acquired or improved
- it should not be used exclusively since it does not consider on-the-job-performance.

HOW NATWEST LIFE ASSURANCE APPRAISES PERFORMANCE

NatWest's Life's business success depends on effective relationships with customers for periods of up to 25 years, and that in turn depends on the effective performance of people in the company. The company's appraisal system therefore reflects behaviour in line with the company's mission which stresses outstanding service delivery and valuing customers, shareholders and staff.

According to the human resources team, 'most companies look at performance in terms of what people have achieved, but we felt it was important to measure and reward inputs, not just outcomes'. Part of the thinking behind this was that it is easy to measure certain outcomes such as sales performance, but what the company calls 'soft areas' such as personnel are more difficult to measure in the same way.

The appraisal system is based on a dual approach. First staff are assessed by their line manager to see whether they have reached or exceeded the standards required in their particular role: the second part of the appraisal looks at behaviour. Overall there are four sets of criteria:

1 How they performed against the areas they were accountable for in their role.
2 How they performed against specific objectives drawn from the company's business plan.
3 The extent to which they have developed the competencies needed in their job.
4 Whether they have worked to achieve the company's vision by

following such guiding principles as: integrity, openness and customer-focus.

To support the developmental process, quarterly meetings are held between individuals and their line managers. These meetings provide opportunities to review development plans and identify the most effective way of meeting individual needs, either internally or externally. These meetings are deliberately informal and no performance score is given, although they are integrated with the annual appraisal.

The appraisal system is part of an overall strategy to ensure that human resource systems reflect the needs of the business at each stage of its development.

INTRODUCING A NEW APPROACH TO APPRAISAL

Key stages in implementation:

- consider changing the name 'appraisal' to one with positive connotations in your organization (examples include People Development, Personal Development Planning etc)
- find out what people think of the current system and what they would like to see in its place
- communicate the changes throughout the organization
- consult everyone who would be involved
- train all those who will carry out the appraisals
- set up workshops, focus groups and attitude surveys to ensure participation and support.

A new approach like this cannot be implemented overnight. It should be introduced with a great deal of consultation to ensure that people understand the changes. It is worth taking time over this stage because their support and participation are crucial to the success of the programme. People throughout the organization need to understand the reason for the new form of appraisal and their role in it.

To ensure effective consultation, consider:

- off-site workshops for senior managers
- facilitated discussions and focus groups for employees
- surveys of employee attitudes
- any other method of ensuring maximum participation.

A completely new approach will require a programme of training for the whole organization. Without this commitment to training, problems arise if team leaders are unable to grasp the purpose of the programme and employees become suspicious of the whole process. Part of this training will need to involve the communication issues that have been at the root of the lack of success of so many traditional appraisal systems.

The object of a good appraisal should be to build on achievements so the opening moments are vital. Both parties need to prepare carefully for the session. The reason for acknowledging successes is threefold:

- to learn from what made the achievement possible
- to build confidence and self esteem so that the areas for improvement can also be turned into achievements
- to encourage an atmosphere of problem solving and create a learning experience.

The appraisors may have to add to the appraisees' view of their successes. They should facilitate the discussion and, by asking open questions and prompting where appropriate, encourage the appraisee to review each achievement to discover what processes and skills had been used to make it happen. The appraisor should acknowledge both the achievement itself and the appraisee's skills in achieving it, before moving on to the next stage: the areas for improvement.

Research has proved that people find it very hard to listen to more than two or three points of critical feedback so it is worth in preparation choosing the most effective areas to work on. It is also crucial at this stage that the appraiser keeps to a form that makes it clear that it is the task that needs to be improved rather than the individual themselves. For example 'the report on ... was rather thin and unthought through. What do you think happened?' rather than, 'You always rush things'.

The tone of the meeting should be open and investigative rather than judgemental. The relationship between the appraisor and appraisee is vital to the success of the process and should concentrate on:

- trust
- support
- confidence
- openness
- a willingness to work towards continual improvement.

Any employee who believes that their appraisor is on their side, working with them to create improved performance and personal development, can achieve miracles. Any other relationship is likely to create an atmosphere where the process is something people do under sufferance with poor results and the process itself will be judged to be ineffective.

CHECKLIST SUMMARY

- The open, consultative and team-based culture in Kaizen organizations – where personnel and HR strategies are linked to business development strategies – requires an equally visible and sharing approach to performance appraising that links individual performance to strategic objectives.

- 'Continuous performance management' (CPM) has largely replaced the single annual performance appraisal meeting typical within more conventional organizations.

- CPM is overtly developmental in nature and driven more by an interest in the *processes* that underpin performance than the outputs generated by the performance.

- CPM is characterized by these qualities:
  - a concern for human factors
  - a link to business needs
  - openness
  - immediacy; that is, it is managed by the people *directly* involved and, it happens all the time, not at a time remote from events
  - the full participatory involvement of both appraisee and appraisor integration with other, training, reward and development opportunities/policies
  - inclusivity; that is, *all* employees participate in the same, single status, appraisal procedure.

- CPM/performance appraising can involve different participants in different system configurations:

  Employee → Employee : Peer appraisal
  Team → Employee : Team appraisal
  Team leader/Manager → Employee : Leader appraisal

善

Team leader/Manager ↔ Employee : 360° appraisal
Employee → Team leader/Manager : Upward appraisal.

- Every system should encourage a willingness to work jointly towards continuous improvement.

11

REWARDING
QUALITY
PEOPLE

改善

'You have to know your organization. If a reward seems to be unthinking or mechanical in the way it's handed out, then it won't work'

(Head of Training, National Health Service)

New ways of working and new methods of appraisal are having an impact on remuneration packages and any organization which seeks to motivate its staff needs to look long and hard at how these packages can support their goals. It is important to consider the question not only of money, but also of other rewards:

- financial rewards
- employee and fringe benefits
- non-financial rewards.

Financial rewards include short-term incentives made up of salary and bonuses while long-term incentives include profit sharing, share ownership and stock options. Financial rewards are not commonly regarded as motivational in the long term but when they are not perceived to be 'fair', they can become demotivating agents.

Employee benefits include insurance cover, pension schemes and sick-pay, while fringe benefits include cars, holidays and company discounts.

Non-financial benefits are more complex and include the

motivational aspects identified in Chapter 9. These are largely intrinsic (ie derived from the job itself) and are mainly self-generated in that people seek the type of work that satisfies them, but can be enhanced by management through giving greater responsibility, development, job design, policies and practices. The factors affecting intrinsic motivation include responsibility, freedom to act, scope to develop and use skills and abilities, interesting and challenging work and opportunities for advancement.

The second aspect of motivation may be called extrinsic in that it is what is done to and for people to motivate them, aspects such as bonus pay, but it also includes non-financial rewards such as praise and recognition. Extrinsic motivators currently in use in the UK include:

- praise (verbal recognition)
- long-service awards
- status symbols
- sabbaticals
- work-related trips abroad
- extra holiday
- travel
- voucher schemes
- catalogue schemes
- luxury gift items
- team recognition (weekends away)
- titles
- office furniture
- secretarial support
- equipment (mobile phones, personal computers etc)
- flexible hours
- degree of supervision
- parking space
- promotion

As can be seen from all the motivators stated, a wide variety of options are available to an organization and no one form of package is guaranteed to be successful. Each organization should consider its culture carefully, what its values and strategy suggest, and consult staff before embarking on a new programme. Once a programme is in place, it is necessary to continually re-evaluate it to check its effectiveness. There is little point in spending large amounts of money on motivators which do not, or no longer, motivate staff.

For many years, sales staff have received a low basic salary with a commission based on their personal sales with a further series of awards available at the end of year depending on how well they have performed in comparison with the rest of their salesforce.

This form of salary plus awards is increasingly popular and is being used for many other types of employee. Cash seems to be losing favour as personnel departments move towards issuing vouchers as a perk or a performance incentive. 'With cash, a bonus is merely added to the pay packet and absorbed into the rest of the money. With vouchers, the employee can purchase something they will always remember', says one manager who runs a voucher scheme. Konica Business Systems also uses vouchers but warns 'for the best staff incentives, you have got to offer something which the person would not normally buy' and admits that they are very flexible and easier to administer than cash but you have to make sure that the employee can exchange them for something that is a motivator.

Organizations benefit from vouchers because they are easy to administer, save the employee NI and Income Tax and provide a gift that can genuinely motivate each individual by providing them with a wide choice of items including vouchers for child-care, travel, groceries, electrical goods, healthcare, education and even wedding expenses!

One organization that uses vouchers successfully is British Alcan who reward hourly-paid staff for good food safety. For an accident-free year, £15,000 worth of vouchers is shared between the staff; if there is one accident, the amount is reduced to £10,000 and to £5,000 if there are two accidents.

The **Automobile Association** (AA) has also found vouchers valuable in achieving its business strategy of the management-employee relationship mirroring that of the customer relationship. To achieve this they have replaced ten layers of management with

▶

four, formed all the 5,500 staff into teams and involved them in a broad programme of training. A new incentive scheme called 'Teamwork pays' was introduced which links the overall perform-ance of the organization with local performance measures on which teams compete in leagues. They receive updated figures monthly so that they maintain their commitment to become a quarterly or annual winner. Winners can elect a team outing from a menu of options or vouchers to a given value. According to the incentives manager 'It's not just the money that counts; it's the recognition'. Teams are as proud of the title of Patrol Team of the Year and the annual presentation ceremony as the awards them-selves and the AA has benefited from both productivity and quality gains at a modest cost. It acknowledges that the major expense is incurred in collating the updated information which gives each team the motivation to improve continuously.

Stating one thing as a principle and rewarding another is guaranteed to cause problems

---

One of the most misunderstood forms of communication is that of example. If a Western organization rewards its employees based, for example, on:

- seniority
- length of service
- individual performance

it is sending a clear message that it values status and loyalty above the achievement of its strategic goals and that anyone who keeps out of trouble as well as impressing senior manage-ment will do well. Paying salary increases for individual per-formance will be unlikely to encourage enhanced team performance as everyone will be trying to optimize their own salary. If a company is organized on team lines, the concept of team pay or team-based bonuses should certainly be considered.

TEAM-BASED PAY

More than 25 per cent of the retail finance companies in the UK are moving into team-based pay according to research by KPMG Peat Marwick Chartered Accountants Management Consultants (KPMG) and Bristol University. It has been suggested that this is to resolve the concern felt for individual performance related pay.

Manufacturing industry has found benefits from introducing team-based pay after it found that teamworking was a solution to many of the difficulties in the motivation of a large unstructured production line. Teamworking provides the family-sized units that enable people to work together better, support each other and provide the personal relationships that make life and work more enjoyable. But if the pay is still based on individual performance, the competitive element is likely to get in the way of overall productivity and quality improvements. Team-based pay has proved to provide the final link to achieving all the above. When each individual is paid on the performance of their own team, the motivation to support each other, make improvement suggestions and plan tasks in the most effective way leaps dramatically.

Team-based pay can also include options for rewarding:

- increased productivity
- increased profits for the organization
- improvement suggestions.

If an organization wants to promote job rotation, it will be unlikely to realize it unless pay for grading can be reassessed, as there will be few volunteers for a system that penalizes them for attempting to widen their experience and knowledge.

There is an increasing need to focus on the person rather than the job

---

A balance needs to be found, allowing pay flexibility for individuals within teams against a framework of expectations about skills, behaviour, loosely-defined roles and outcomes.

Recently there has been a huge increase in organizations widening their salary/grade band levels with additional funds available for rewarding skills and knowledge acquisition and other desirable measures to send the message that contribution and flexibility are from now on more important to driving pay than grade alone. This approach has often been very successful, particularly in organizations that want to respond quickly to market changes and where person/role flexibility is desirable.

The implications of broader banding with bonuses are:

- promotion is less frequent and more significant when it does occur
- people's expectations have to be managed so that they are prepared to accept moves without promotion
- new salary progression rules have to be developed, because not everyone will reach the ceiling level over time
- pay communication is more focused on individual salary level than pay range.

This approach is not appropriate to every organization; this is currently an area of experimentation, and organizations need to consider which approach may be most appropriate to their goals.

One simple approach to changing pay levels to encourage the development of additional skills and qualifications is to pay for their achievement (for example, the retail sector is increasingly paying for National Vocational Qualifications (NVQs). If your organization states that it believes people become more valuable to it as they acquire and then use newly identified skills or competencies, then rewarding their achievement makes a powerful contribution to motivation.

Increased productivity

Many organizations make additional payments to teams for production over and above agreed target levels. Other groups allow teams to leave work early when they have completed their targets and in some companies, this has meant some teams working only a four day week. Each option will have different implications in different organizations and will need to be assessed carefully. It is also important to agree fair and reasonable targets and allow some form of autonomy as to how they are produced. Flexi-time working is often very attractive to staff and, so long as it does not cause difficulties to other production units, it can pay long-term dividends.

Increased profits for the organization

Many organizations have a profit-sharing system with employees based on the premise that 'what you do is what makes us the profit, so we will share it with you'. Others feels that if employees are paid a fair wage then the profit should be wholly ploughed back into the organization and its infrastructure. But recent outrage among the public about UK senior executives' pay while members of their staff are being made redundant is likely to lead to a call for more shared profits with employees as well as customers.

Fair pay?

There are two main criteria that an employee unconsciously uses to assess whether they think they are being paid fairly:

- Whether they are paid a 'market' rate compared to others both in their organization and outside doing similar work
- What their superiors (immediate managers as well as senior managers) are being paid.

During the 1980s in the UK, the first criterion remained fairly stable as those with skills and marketable qualities were sought widely and organizations had to pay the going rate to keep good staff. Some lower grades have fallen in terms of rates and this has tended to be seen throughout all industries. But the second set of criteria has changed dramatically. In 1991, *USA Today* revealed that CEOs in the USA earned eighty-five times as much as the average worker, in Great Britain thirty-three times, in Germany twenty-five times and in Japan seventeen times. It is believed that the rate in Britain is rising still and while employees are being laid off, this is causing great concern to Government as well as the general public. An organization that genuinely wants to motivate its staff and produce quality products and services may do well to consider how to create a remuneration structure that is felt by all staff to be fair.

Is there anything we can learn from Japanese companies about rewards and motivation?

Not according to Tetsuo Mizuno who heads Square, a games software house in Tokyo. A traditional Japanese organization pays salaries based on seniority with occasionally a team element (more common in sales in department stores) and one week annual holiday in the summer (staff are entitled to more but rarely expected to take it). In the fast-changing world in which all organizations are now operating, the Japanese are increasingly looking to the West for examples of motivational reward programmes.

Tetsuo Mizuno's Square does not limit recruitment to university graduates – 80 per cent of the staff have held other jobs, including teaching and acting. Their main criterion is that they should be inventive and competent. They have one month summer holiday and an additional 20 days of paid holiday during which they are encouraged to travel and experience new things. They also need not keep official office hours; so long as they touch base each day and are productive, they are encouraged to work flexibly. The evaluation system is a mixture of the Western merit approach and the Japanese lifetime employment system. Square's spectacular results in productivity and morale are likely to lead to more innovation of the rewards system in Japan.

A more fruitful source of ideas is the USA, where a growing number of organizations are changing their ownership structure to give employees a genuine stake in their profits and future.

SATURN CORPORATION

Saturn Corporation, a wholly owned subsidiary of General Motors in a special partnership with United Auto Workers, started production in 1990 with a commitment to train all team members, build leadership qualities, compensate everyone fairly and offer strong employee incentives. To develop a compensation plan for its teams, Saturn investigated other organizations' packages and devised a Risk and Reward programme, made up of base pay, risk pay and reward pay.

Base pay is lower than the market rate – that's the risk part; it started at 5 per cent and has grown slowly to 10 per cent. Team members can, with reward pay, earn considerably more than the market rate.

Because the employees are prepared to take the risk in return for a genuine share of the profitability of the organization, both sides feel it is fair. But the HR manager warns that the system is working because it is part of the completely integrated process including:

- self-managed teams
- a minimum of 92 training hours per employee annually
- a genuine involvement between management and staff

and that it probably would fail if introduced purely as a reward system. Saturn report their results on a quarterly basis so that there is an awareness of what is happening and staff are involved in decision making and are familiar with organizational budgets.

Communication and openness seem also to be key elements to the success of their system.

PEPSICO

PepsiCo, with 450,000 employees and operations in 166 countries, is determined to act and feel like a small company. To support this, the HR department has created a system to empower all levels of workers as well as rewarding long service. They have introduced an employee share option programme – with a difference – called 'Share Power'. The organization grants stock options each year to *all* full-time employees based on 10 per cent of their previous year's salary. The stocks are 20 per cent exerciseable each year, meaning that they are fully vested after five years, with ten years to exercise their options. This can mean a sizeable nest egg for a long-term employee. The programme provides a strong incentive for every employee to act as an entrepreneur and there are many examples of both individual and team performance achievements. 'Share Power' seems to be helping PepsiCo show a genuine commitment to sharing power with its employees.

SPRINGFIELD REMANUFACTURING CORPORATION

Springfield Remanufacturing Corporation in Missouri have an ESOP where employees own 32 per cent of the company's stock and have introduced 'The Great Game of Business' to ensure that they play their part fully in the organization's success. They spend nearly five times as much on business and financial training for all employees, which starts on their first day at work, as job-related skills training. Each Wednesday, 40 or 50 members of staff meet to play the 'game' which includes each person sharing the income and expense figures for their department for that week and reporting back from other employees. The organization believes that a combination of the training and the 'game' has led to the average 15 per cent annual rise in profits as it helps 'employees understand and realize what part they play in the business and how they can make a difference'. An additional spin-off has been that SRC has created many entrepreneurs who have used their share options and financial help from SRC to set up their own businesses in which SRC shares in the profits estimated in 1995 at $15 million.

PHELPS COUNTY BANK

Phelps County Bank founded in 1963 in Missouri as a small pri-
vately-owned bank prided itself on its friendly customer care and
in the 1970s grew rapidly and began to attract the attention of
larger banks keen to swallow it up. The owner decided to launch
an Employee Share Option Programme to help maintain its inde-
pendence. Now the holding company is 100 per cent owned by
the 65 employees, with the ESOP contributions 25 per cent of pay,
even though other staff compensations remain higher than those
of its competitors. Phelps have achieved this through increased
profits and the share price has increased more than fivefold over
the past l5 years, about double the rise of its competitors.

Phelps are committed to teamworking, communication, training
and development and together with the increased sense of 'ownership' by the staff, are a classic example of a small company producing excellent results through excellent service to the
customers. Emma Lou Brent, the CEO, says 'If you have 55
employees who really understand banking and who constantly
watch the bottom line, you're a lot less likely to have problems.
Employee ownership isn't about a few people skimming the
cream. This is about creating a lot more cream by allowing everyone to share in its production and the results'.

REWARDING EMPLOYEE SUGGESTIONS

At the heart of Kaizen is the principle that it is the many hundreds of thousands of small improvements that make the difference between quality and indifference and that it is the
individual who actually does the work who best knows how it
can be improved.

The problem for Western organizations has been how to find
out from the employee what it is that might make a difference
to their work and so affect the organization as a whole.
Obviously payment reward for productivity increases and part-

ownership in the organization and its profits have their part to play, but many organizations have discovered that a small payment for each worthwhile suggestion can increase motivation to come up with them.

Payment for suggestions can include:

- a small sum for every suggestion made
- a larger sum for any suggestion implemented
- a share in the savings made by a suggestion
- a share in royalties for any further marketing of the suggestion.

There are advantages and disadvantages to each of these options.

Pay for each suggestion made

Can result in huge quantities of suggestions, many of which are impractical, duplicated or simply foolish. Some organizations have been forced to ask their staff to test each suggestion and show their research, before they can claim a reward.

Pay for each suggestion implemented

Can cause difficulties in judging who or which team has ownership of the suggestion itself.

Payment based on the savings of each suggestion

This takes time as the savings may take many months to be fully revealed and can cause similar difficulties to the item above – exactly who is responsible for the idea.

Payment based on royalties earned from a suggestion

A classic example of this is the man who suggested a tilting deck on an aircraft carrier to save fuel and facilitate the take-off of planes. The courts eventually decided in his favour and he now shares royalties from foreign navies who have followed the idea.

This raises the question of exactly what does the salary cover – just payment for a job or all the ideas and suggestions the individual is capable of. Much discussion and thought needs to be given to this topic before any sensible guidelines suitable for a particular organization can be formulated.

CHECKLIST SUMMARY

- salary needs to be in line with the stated values of the organization

- rewards systems need to be appropriate to the requirements of the organization

- employees need to be part of the process of deciding appropriate reward systems

- training and development should never be part of a reward package; they should complement it

- employees need to feel that they are being rewarded fairly for their contribution.

CONCLUDING COMMENTS

'For the want of a nail, the shoe was lost
For the want of a shoe, the horse was lost
For the want of a horse, the general was lost
For the want of a general, the army was lost
For the want of an army, the battle was lost
For the want of a battle, the war was lost
For the want of a war, the country was lost
And all for the sake of a nail.'

Within this old poem lies one of the principles of Kaizen: that it is generally the smallest things that cause the biggest disasters. It is nearly always the straw that breaks the camel's back rather than a heavy load.

Kaizen tells us that only by being constantly aware and making hundreds of thousands of small improvements, is it possible to produce goods and services of genuine quality, that will satisfy customers.

And that this is most easily achieved through the involvement, motivation and continual development of each and every employee in the organization.

And that this involvement of the staff is dependent on the commitment of the senior management, a clear strategy and perserverance – because it is not a quick fix but a continual on-going process that creates the desired results.

The Europe Japan Centre is committed to the idea of encouraging a broad creative environment within organizations, by using the building blocks of Kaizen core values in an integrated way rather than imposing isolated tools (such as Total Quality Management). This is because it understands that Kaizen is a *Total Concept* rather than a menu out of which you can pick the bits you like best and still expect it to deliver the benefits you require.

The Europe Japan Centre defines a creative organization as one which:

- is not afraid to act
- responds flexibly and quickly
- accepts failure as part of the process
- challenges accepted 'wisdom'
- is committed to learning
- communicates with markets and people
- develops and involves people
- celebrates success

'If you're not failing, you're not trying .'

Einstein

So often the West takes on new management tools and techniques because it is looking for an answer that will make everything easy. They are often only prepared to make a commitment to an answer that works in the short term so that in the long term they have nothing to worry about.

One of the truths that has come to us from the East, is that there are no easy, quick-fix answers. The only guaranteed path to excellence is slow and sure with no winning post at the end. Excellence is a never ending journey.

It is also important to remember that, although perhaps a struggle at the start, the process generally creates its own momentum; it is by trusting and setting free the most important capital assets of any organization, the employees, that the management and HR department may well find that the path to excellence becomes easier as more and more people are committed to removing the obstacles that emerge on the way. It is the setting free and the trusting that may be the most difficult part of the process for management and it is in this area that this book has sought to provide guidelines and examples to show the way.

THE ROUTE MAP

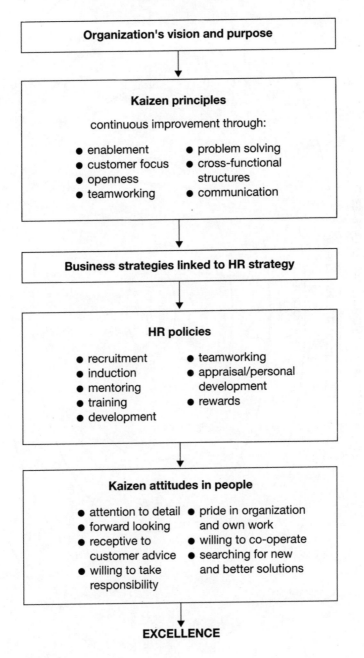

Organization's vision and purpose

Kaizen principles

continuous improvement through:

- enablement
- customer focus
- openness
- teamworking
- problem solving
- cross-functional structures
- communication

Business strategies linked to HR strategy

HR policies

- recruitment
- induction
- mentoring
- training
- development
- teamworking
- appraisal/personal development
- rewards

Kaizen attitudes in people

- attention to detail
- forward looking
- receptive to customer advice
- willing to take responsibility
- pride in organization and own work
- willing to co-operate
- searching for new and better solutions

EXCELLENCE

改

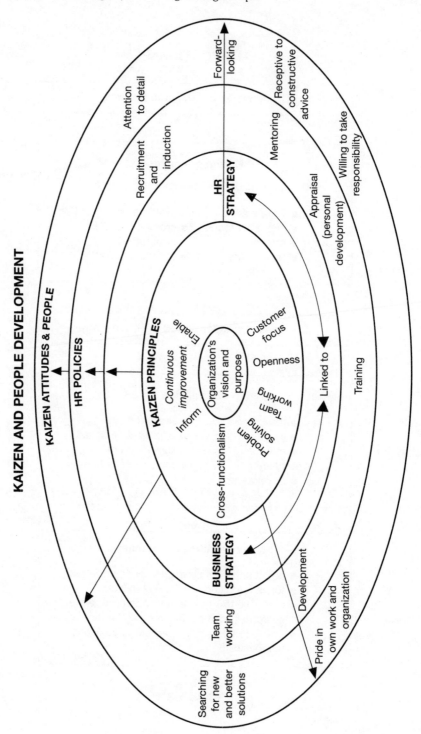

As indicated in various parts of this book, however, the Kaizen route to winning through people can give rise to a number of problems, some of which may need considerable resourcefulness to overcome. Problems may include:

- overcoming middle management resistance: if some of the authority traditionally exercised by middle managers in the West passes to team leaders, middle managers naturally feel threatened that their role will be eliminated. This need not be the case, if, for example, the traditional role of middle management is shifted to a more strategic role and they take on part of the responsibility for championing and driving the Kaizen approach.

- overcoming union worries and fears: again a union's role in a company that adopts Kaizen will ideally become less confrontational. If management is prepared to be more open, union representatives can take on a more participatory role. Management also needs to be aware of the impact of changing work practices associated with Kaizen-type organizations (people may fear they are working themselves out of a job, or that older people may be forced out in favour of younger ones), and deal explicitly with them.

- overcoming disappointment at never achieving perfection: inherent in Kaizen is the fact that as soon as a new standard is achieved, a higher one should be sought. Unless the benefits of higher achievement are made clear, and efforts made to ensure employees share in the gains, the process can become demotivating rather than motivating.

- overcoming a lack of time: the time needed to change attitudes, to put in place new practices, and to improve communications should not be underestimated. People throughout an organization, including senior managers, will need to examine how they should spend their time most effectively, in order to devote sufficient effort to effecting change and promoting Kaizen.

- maintaining the momentum: unless Kaizen becomes a natural, rather than an enforced, way of life, it will always be difficult to keep the momentum going. There needs to be a real shift in culture within an organization, or gains made will all too easily slip back. A positive management style which encourages and rewards flexibility, participation and creative thinking can play a major role, as can:
  - constant communication
  - involvement
  - training and development
  - measurement
  - a no-blame culture
  - recognition and rewards
  - customer and supplier contact for employees as well as managers.

Two final words of caution. Firstly, too many organizations have tried to impose a Japanese form of Kaizen on their workforce and been surprised that it has been resented and produced disappointing results. Any process must be adapted to both the nation's and the individual organization's culture to be taken on and implemented effectively. A genuinely effective process needs to be adapted and altered until it fits the organization like a second skin – so that no one is really aware that it has put it on, that it lives and moves with the wearer.

Secondly, what the Japanese most envy about the West is the creativity and innovation which have been produced by the culture of individuality. The challenge for the West is to adopt the advantages of Kaizen but at the same time create structures which promote innovation, in order to provide the best of both the East and the West. Experience of partnerships of Western and Japanese organizations leads to the conclusion that there need be no conflict between the two, or that the conflict can be creative. As the West has found in the past, innovation rarely claims to be the final answer; it is the organizations who market and perfect new products and services who have often reaped the gains, and the inventors who have often been disappointed that they have not been allowed to continue their work.

Finally, organizations may like to establish to what extent they are following strategies and encouraging behaviour that are likely to help them follow the Kaizen approach effectively. Some of the questions that may help you clarify your thoughts include:

HEALTHCHECK FOR ORGANIZATIONS WHICH AIM TO WIN THROUGH PEOPLE

Vision

- Does your organization have a vision?
- Does everyone know about it?
- Does it inspire them?

Statement of Purpose

- Does your organization have a statement of purpose?
- Does everyone know about it?
- Do most people act in line with it?
- Is it up-to-date?
- Were a cross-section of people involved in creating it?

HR Strategy

- Do you have a comprehensive HR strategy?
- Is it up-to-date?
- Does everyone know what it says?
- Is it linked to your business strategy?

Principles

- Are you involved in

continuous improvement activities

teamworking

problem-solving activities

cross-functional activities

- Do you enable employees to make decisions in their own areas of work?

Customers

- Do all employees know what customers think about your products and services?
- Do employees have a chance to meet customers directly?
- Do employees receive regular feedback on customers?
- Do employees hear praise, as well as criticism, from customers?

Team leadership

- Do your team leaders act as leaders, rather than supervisors?
- Do they create an atmosphere of trust, openness and improvement?
- Do they encourage a participatory and no-blame culture?
- Are they effective motivators?

Teams

- Do team members work co-operatively together?
- Do you allow regular time for team meetings?
- Do you measure the success of teams according to criteria developed by the teams?

Recruitment

- Do you involve the people who will be working with the new recruit?
- Does the recruitment process reflect your values?

Induction

- Does your induction process reflect your values?

- Does it include personal, as well as job and company, induction?
- Does it include the 'bigger picture' (the company visions, aims etc)?
- Do you include part-time and homeworkers in your induction?
- Is induction taken seriously? Does it last for more than a half day?

Training and development

- Do all employees have their own training and development plans?
- Do you seek to widen the skills and knowledge of all employees?
- Do you encourage employees to develop skills and knowledge which are not directly work-related?
- Does your training include 'softer' skills, such as communication and working well in teams?
- Do you 'embed' training, by encouraging use of new knowledge and by spreading one person's knowledge to the team of department?

Appraisals

- Do you use appraisals mainly as a means to develop people?
- Is your appraisals process perceived as fair, open and relevant?
- Do you practice upward, as well as downward, appraisal?

Rewards

- Do you ensure people feel valued, and rewarded for any extraordinary contributions?
- Do you share the gains made by improved products, services or ways of working?
- Is your reward system perceived as fair?

Communications

- Are employees aware of the vision and the business plan, and of their roles within the overall plan?
- Do you make efforts to communicate directly, rather than letting the grapevine take over?

- Are employees able to communicate their ideas easily?
- Do you always respond to employees' ideas?
- Is the number of good ideas and suggestions increasing?
- Do you have effective and regular communication across your organization?

Organizational leadership

- Do you spend enough time on creating the future, rather than dealing with day-to-day problems?
- Do you communicate the organization's vision clearly, regularly and with enthusiasm?
- Do you spend time regularly 'walking the job'?
- Do you work as a management team?
- Do you delegate as much as is possible?
- Do you encourage Kaizen through your own practice, as well as your words?

The greater the number of 'yes' answers, the closer your organization is likely to be to creating a culture in which you can truly win through people.

INDEX

Also from Pitman Publishing

KAIZEN STRATEGIES FOR SUCCESSFUL LEADERSHIP

Tony Barnes

What will the organisation of tomorrow look like? What will be the role of leaders in these organisations? What characteristics will you need to have and how should you apply your skills?

Kaizen Strategies for Successful Leadership develops and extends the philosophy of Kaizen for use in the West:

- Tap the ideas, innovations and creativity of your people.
- Inspire your people with a vision of the future.
- Make your organisation an 'education unit' where continuous improvement is a natural part of life.
- Share the role of management and encourage internal entrepreneurs.

Using case studies from organisations of all sizes in the East & West, who have already discovered the power of Kaizen, this book will help you become an effective leader for now and the future.

ISBN 0 273 61709 5   Price £25.00

Available through all good bookshops

Prices are subject to change without notice

Also from Pitman Publishing

KAIZEN STRATEGIES FOR CUSTOMER CARE

Pat Wellington

Throughout the world companies are realising that their success depends largely on the satisfaction of their customers. Many conventional customer care programmes are failing to provide this satisfaction.

This is where Kaizen strategies can make a vital difference. This approach (adapted to suit western national and business cultures) goes way beyond the cheery smile or even a genuine desire to please. It embeds a fundamental values and cultural change within an organization.

Guidelines are given on how to introduce Kaizen principles into your organisation and make them work; the ultimate objective being to show how you can improve your organization's bottom line by enhancing internal and external relations.

ISBN : 0 273 61472 X　　　　　　　　　　Price £25.00

Available through all good bookshops

Prices are subject to change without notice

Europe Japan Centre Training Programmes

All Europe Japan Centre programmes are individually tailored. Tuition is in small groups and is highly participative. The list below provides an indication of our main areas of expertise.

Awareness Sessions

Kaizen and Creativity
What is Kaizen and how can it be combined with Western creativity to form an unbeatable approach

Leadership of Tomorrow
The new role of senior management in creating world-class companies

Research and Consultancy

Our unique research programme (R&I) assesses the current state of your organization and begins the vital process of involving staff more fully

One-to-one sessions with senior managers provide advice and support on cultural change or particular aspects

Our consultants can work alongside your teams to advise on organizational and human resources changes

Seminars and Workshops to Develop Skills and Put Theory into Action

Implementing Kaizen

How to introduce a culture of continuous improvement, building on the strengths of your organization

From Managers to Leaders

How to inspire and develop your people

The Kaizen Approach to Customer Care

Using Kaizen to enhance your service to customers

Developing Effective Team Leaders

How team leaders can get the most from their teams in terms of productivity, efficiency and creativity

Creating Teams that Work

How to put together the right people, set guidelines, organize meetings and create results

Inter-team Co-operation

How to break down barriers between departments and work more efficiently across the whole organization

The Kaizen Toolbox

Practical tools and statistical techniques, from brainstorming to PDCA and Pareto analysis, to measure performance and improvements

The Kaizen Approach to Problem Solving

How to identify real problems, analyze their root causes and find creative solutions

Personal Development and Kaizen

Workshops to build the personal skills needed to embed Kaizen in the behaviour of everyone in your organization

Seminars and workshops can be arranged for all levels, from directors and senior managers to team leaders and team members.

Europe Japan Centre Services also include research on the Japanese market and Japan Briefings.

For further information or an informal meeting contact Pat Wellington or Catherine Davis at:

The Europe Japan Centre,
Nash House, St. George Street, London W1R 9DE.
Tel: 0171–491 1791   Fax: 0171–491 4055